Why the Best Are the Best

I have always enjoyed reading anything that Kevin has shared and Why the Best Are the Best *is no different. Kevin has a unique way of taking the most important components of success—leadership, team building, and personal development—and simplifying them to the point that we can immediately insert them into our lives, careers, and teams. Along the way, he will stretch your thinking so that you can find ways to refine your success plan for you or your team.*

JAY WRIGHT
Head Coach, Villanova University
NCAA Champion 2016, 2018

I have known Kevin for a long time and have seen him work in many situations. He has worked with NBA all-stars, Hall of Fame players, and thirteen- to fifteen-year-olds wanting to make their high school teams. In every situation, he has worked to make them better and cared equally about the person, regardless of stature. The lessons he shares in this book will help you whether you are with a sports team, a corporate team or someone just trying to improve! Why the Best Are the Best *will help you get there!*

ROY WILLIAMS
Head Coach, University of North Carolina
NCAA Champion 2005, 2009, 2017
Basketball Hall of Fame Inductee

I am so pleased that Kevin Eastman has written his book, Why the Best Are the Best. *Kevin is among the finest teachers of the game that I have ever known. He personifies what General Martin Dempsey calls the three most important principles of leadership: character, competence, and humility. Kevin is the most curious learner I have known and is an expert in his craft of coaching and teaching. His humility is inspiring, as is his willingness to share his knowledge. His study of what makes one the best is a comprehensive guide on how we can be our best selves in whatever we do.*

I am extraordinarily lucky to have learned so much from Kevin over the years. I know his book will do for you what Kevin has done for me: provide the tools to motivate and inspire you to thoughtfully pursue excellence. That's what the very best coaches and teachers do, and that is exactly what Kevin Eastman is: the very best coach and teacher.

JAY BILAS
ESPN Basketball Analyst

Kevin draws from his vast experiences in his book Why the Best Are the Best. *His relationships in sports and business, and his passion for education, are seen throughout this book as he offers an effective strategy for personal and team growth. Each chapter is laced with "wisdom bombs" making this a compulsory read for teams in any sport and teams in the ever-competitive corporate world as well.*

GEORGE RAVELING
Former College Basketball Head Coach
Basketball Hall of Fame Inductee

Kevin is one of the best speakers and teachers I have come across in the profession. If you want to learn more about leadership, coaching, self-motivation, or taking your team or yourself to the next level of performance, this book is a must read.

ERIK SPOELSTRA
Head Coach, Miami Heat
NBA Champion 2012, 2013

Kevin Eastman came to our school district at a time of transition. I had just been hired as the new superintendent in the middle of the year and Kevin's presentation and manner was exactly what our district needed. He was a keynote speaker to a professional development day and spoke to an auditorium of 500 educators. His relationship with the audience was immediate. His message of the power of words and the value he placed upon the role of teachers in young peoples' lives was impactful. Kevin's writing reinforces and dives deep into concepts around intentionally being a better version of ourselves. Living and preparing with intention every single day is such a potent reminder for everyone. Kevin Eastman affected my own development as a new superintendent, as a coach of people, as a parent of young women, as a wife, and as a daughter. His message carries throughout our roles as human beings.

GINA THOMPSON
Superintendent, Yuma Union High School District
Yuma, Arizona

If you want practicality and guidance, this book is for you. It hits the bullseye for those who are ready to elevate their game on the playing field of life. Whether you are an athlete, a corporate titan, a teacher, a salesperson, or a non-profit professional, this book will give you the tools to be a champion. Chapter 3's "The Champion's Compass" is proof that Kevin Eastman is a lifelong learner—an attribute of any leader I'd want to follow. His conversational, storytelling style makes this book a great read!

REBECCA POWERS
Founder, Impact Austin

Kevin is a one-of-a-kind coach and leader. His examples of what high performance looks like in the sports world translate in amazing ways to business and life in general. I have seen Kevin talk to groups of kids, business leaders, and to my own team. Every time I am amazed by his energy, passion, clarity, and how he connects with each group. My only regret when he speaks is that I wish we had more time with him. Now, with this book, we can have Kevin's words and stories anytime we want. I intend to make this my gift of the year to those I want to inspire.

SANFORD D. SIGAL
President and CEO, NewMark Merrill Companies

I have known Kevin for forty-five years and his dedication to excellence is the same today as it was back then. It quickly became apparent to all of us on the team that his discipline, humility, and incredible work ethic would carry him to great accomplishments. No one outmatched Kevin. I have zero doubt that if he had not become a world-class basketball coach, motivator, and trainer, that he would have become a world-class business executive. Even back in 1973, he embraced, embodied, and more importantly, lived those twenty-five words.

BOB MCCURDY
VP/Corporate Sales, Beasley Media Group

I've seen Kevin in many settings and positions over the years. He is the ultimate learner and has a true willingness to share what he learns. Rest assured he has put tremendous thought to his book, Why the Best Are the Best. *This book will challenge you and show you how to get all you can out of the potential you have. I guarantee you will be pulling excerpts from this book to use with yourself, your family, your teams, your teammates, or even your direct reports as you try to set the course for individual and team improvement.*

LAWRENCE FRANK
President of Basketball Operations, Los Angeles Clippers

WHY

THE BEST ARE THE

BEST

25 POWERFUL WORDS
THAT IMPACT, INSPIRE, AND DEFINE
CHAMPIONS

WHY
THE BEST ARE THE
BEST

KEVIN EASTMAN

WITH FOREWORD BY DOC RIVERS

Published by Advantage, Charleston, South Carolina.
Member of Advantage Media Group.

ADVANTAGE is a registered trademark, and the Advantage colophon is a trademark of Advantage Media Group, Inc.

Printed in the United States of America.

10 9 8 7

ISBN: 978-1-64225-025-1
LCCN: 2018949591

Book design by Carly Blake.

This publication is designed to provide accurate and authoritative information in regard to the subject matter covered. It is sold with the understanding that the publisher is not engaged in rendering legal, accounting, or other professional services. If legal advice or other expert assistance is required, the services of a competent professional person should be sought.

Advantage Media Group is proud to be a part of the Tree Neutral® program. Tree Neutral offsets the number of trees consumed in the production and printing of this book by taking proactive steps such as planting trees in direct proportion to the number of trees used to print books. To learn more about Tree Neutral, please visit **www.treeneutral.com**.

Advantage Media Group is a publisher of business, self-improvement, and professional development books and online learning. We help entrepreneurs, business leaders, and professionals share their Stories, Passion, and Knowledge to help others Learn & Grow. Do you have a manuscript or book idea that you would like us to consider for publishing? Please visit **advantagefamily.com** or call **1.866.775.1696**.

To Wendy and Jake:
I am so lucky to have both of you in my life!

TABLE OF CONTENTS

FOREWORD

As leaders and coaches, we are all in constant pursuit of greatness. It has been proven time and time again that in order to achieve success, you must study the most elite performers in the world. It is from this blueprint that you can create a foundation to form your own personal goals and strategy for success.

From my early days working with Kevin, it was obvious that he was consumed with finding the best practices to not only help himself to get to the next level, but also help our team. Whether it was the most recent article, a video or show, or his endless notes from books he'd read, he was able to compile this information to help the team learn and apply these practices. He was constantly giving me, and our team, ideas, strategies, and teaching points that led to our great success.

As our team began to achieve success, and Kevin continued to add to our habits and mindset, he was instrumental in helping us cultivate Championship DNA. His thirst to learn and his tireless work ethic left no stone unturned when working to create a championship environment. His background from coaching, working with Nike Elite Youth Basketball, and even working in the front office has intertwined him with some of the world's most successful leaders and performers in both sports and business. Kevin has taken all of his experiences and moments with the most diverse groups to find common themes that truly impact and inspire.

Kevin's constant pursuit of knowledge and his diligent research of the best of the best in both sports and business has helped elevate some of the most successful people, teams, and organizations. His ability to take ideas from all his research and give you simple words that hold incredible value is a gift. His passion for helping others has led him to share the most important principles that embody Championship DNA.

Kevin has been instrumental in my success throughout my coaching career, and I am confident this book will help propel you to reach your goals as an individual or a team.

Doc Rivers
Head Coach, LA Clippers
May 2018

Kevin Defines
The 25 Power Words

TRUTH

The ultimate "must have" for personal and team success; without it we'll live in the world of frustration and regret.

ACTION

The only way to get there is to start now.

INTENTIONAL

What I do on purpose to fulfill my purpose.

PREPARATION

I have to be there before I get there.

ACCOUNTABILITY

My word to the team that I will understand, execute,
and hold myself to all I must do to contribute to the
successful completion of our goal.

TRUST

The glue that holds the connection together in order to succeed.

SACRIFICE

Giving up something that may be best for you
but not what's best for the team.

DISCIPLINE

The focused mindset that gets me past mad, sad, and hard.

COMMITMENT

The strength of my word, the back of my teammate,
and the best interest of my team in mind at all times.

BELIEF

The power created inside of me from the work, thought,
research, and preparation I put in behind it.

UNREQUIRED

The work that others don't see, don't think about,
and won't do that I must make a priority.

CHOICES

If I listen to the right voices, I tend to make the right choices.

CIRCLES

The people I allow in to impact my future and the person I become.

COMPETITION

A "given," if I am pursuing greatness; something I must be prepared for and willing to do every day.

PASSION

That pull inside of me that comes from the love I have for something; the emotion that pushes me past the impossible.

HABITS

The good ones are the most powerful and most needed; they are hard to create and difficult to break.

URGENCY

Now wins more often than tomorrow.

STANDARDS

The level of expectation I put on myself, my teammates, and the team; the measurement for filling my capability gap.

COURAGE
The strength that comes from knowing I have done all I can
to take that unknown or uncomfortable step.

CURIOSITY
Knowing that I don't know what I need to know in order to
get me where I want to go.

RESPECT
Giving it keeps me humble; getting it requires earning it.

ADJUSTMENT
Darn, it ain't working!; The "different" next step I must take
to achieve my goal.

HUMILITY
Makes me open and available to keep learning; I don't know it all.

INVESTMENT
All the big and little things I do now that may not reap
a benefit today but will add up to create the opportunity
for success tomorrow.

TALENT
Overrated, unless we add an e and a d; in my world
the e and the d stand for "extra dimension."

How a Skinny Kid from New Jersey Wound up Coaching World Champions

I f you know me at all, you might know me as a basketball coach. That's what I did for more than thirty-five years. I'm not a celebrity or a household name, but I have been around many who are, and I have observed and studied them. I've spent years coaching the best basketball players in the world in the NBA. Before that I spent decades, as a head coach and as an assistant coach at the college level, developing young players—and young human beings.

That's my resume. It doesn't matter a whole lot except for the experience of spending my adult life helping to build champions. Those are some of the credentials that allowed me to participate in success and eventually write this book. In all the ways that really matter, I'm probably a lot like you. Throughout my youth and the early years of my professional life, I was a shy, introverted, skinny kid, who maybe

> *The story that really allows me to write this book is how that introverted, skinny kid from New Jersey worked his way up to be an assistant coach on an NBA world championship team.*

tipped the scale at 162 pounds as a six foot three senior in high school. I lacked self-confidence and doubted my talent. To make up for that self-doubt, I made sure I outworked, out-prepared, and out-hustled everyone else on my teams. The story that really allows me to write this book is how that introverted, skinny kid from New Jersey worked his way up to be an assistant coach on an NBA World Championship team and earned a place in that locker room.

Do you still doubt that we have something in common? Ask yourself these questions.

Do you ever ...

- Doubt your qualifications?
- Fear failure?
- Feel like you have to prove yourself every day?
- Feel like you're not as prepared as you need to be even though you've done nothing *but* prepare?
- Think everyone else is smarter than you?
- Question whether you're as good as your competitor?
- Wonder if you're doing a good enough job, let alone a great job?

Well, join the club! I have felt all these things, especially in my early years in coaching.

The key question I keep asking myself is this: Did this mindset help me get where I am in my career, or did it keep me from climbing faster or higher? I haven't come up with all the answers, but I've kept looking for ways to continue to grow and improve as well as for the means to help me take on each new challenge.

What I can tell you with certainty is that I never would have had the opportunity to enter that world champion's locker room if I hadn't tried to do things I didn't know I could do and if I hadn't committed myself to always working harder than anyone else around me. My accomplishments are because of one simple word: "Try." Try is not one of the 25 Power Words that are the focus of this book. But it could be. You will be amazed at what you can accomplish if you just try.

Growing up, that word was always a way of asking the question: "Can I do this?" *Try* became—and remains—one of those mini-challenges that I believe keeps me sharp and keeps that uneasiness in my stomach that I would get just before game time. It's that feeling of healthy concern—what some might label healthy "fear"—which gave me the urgency to tackle what was next.

Accomplishing anything, overcoming any challenge, requires a start. And starting something requires a willingness to try. So, *try* always precedes *start* in my way of thinking.

Trying, taking on new challenges, facing the unknown, come down to these questions:

- Is my *try* greater than my fear?
- Is my *try* greater than my doubt?
- Is my *try* greater than any embarrassment that I may suffer because I did not accomplish what I set out to do?

To start requires that you get up and get into whatever it is you are trying to accomplish. Success and accomplishment are not about being a spectator, they are about jumping in and being a participant. My simple definition of the word try is this: a decision followed by an effort to accomplish something. The operative word for me is effort.

> *If you* want *to be*
> *successful at anything,*
> *the first step you have*
> *to take is the* try to!

Try and never quit!

If you *want to* be successful at anything, the first step you have to take is the *try to*!

I've told you about the importance the word has for me because, in order for you to get the most from this book, it's important to tell you something about who I am, not just what I did. I come from a "yours, mine, and ours" family as it was known then—what we now call a "blended" family. How we got to be that way is a sad story. My biological mother committed suicide when I was six, leaving behind three boys under the age of ten. Joe, Denny, and I moved with our dad to an apartment in South Jersey where we spent a lot of time on our own while dad worked. Around this time, another family faced a similar tragedy. A father died, leaving behind his wife and six children. Our father and their mother met, later married, and combined the families (our own version of *The Brady Bunch*). The new team brought together six boys and three girls, and I was right in the middle. A few years later, another brother (the "ours") joined us to make ten siblings.

There were so many voices filling the house and people running around to different events that it seemed like there wasn't opportunity for me to do much talking. As a result, I did a lot more thinking and observing. Even though I didn't realize it at the time, I was always in think mode, involved in my own self-talk. I'm sure I've blocked some of the memories of my mother, and certainly, at six, I did not understand my mother's suicide, but one result was that I became the sort of kid who often chose to "go it alone." For some reason, even with all that activity, I often felt lonely. Not bad, not good. It was just how it was for me. Then basketball came along and filled that void ... and ultimately became my love. Through basketball I learned how to work for something bigger than myself.

> *Through basketball I learned how to work for something bigger than myself.*

I fell in love with basketball in junior high school back in Haddonfield, NJ. Once my attention turned to basketball, I thought about the game constantly: how to improve my left hand, how to make a shot off the dribble. What drills could I do to be as good as the other players in town? How could I be a good teammate? And as time went on, there were new questions. How can I help this team win a championship? How can I help set an example through my leadership?

I always lived with a comparative mindset. I always doubted myself. I knew I was working my tail off but didn't know if it was enough. I constantly wondered, "Can I do this?" "Am I good enough?"

Because I was so focused on *try*, I was more committed to improving at basketball than being caught up in the social life of a teenager. The only lighted court (really just a basket and some concrete) in my hometown of Haddonfield was down by the railroad tracks. In junior high we had a big dance every Friday night at seven o'clock, and I'd be late or might not make it at all because I had to get my shots and dribble drills in first. I probably had no shot at ever getting a date because the ball was more important than any dance. Little did I know then that I would be glad that I asked that ball out every Friday—because it has provided a rich and daily learning experience through playing and coaching a game I love.

My commitment began paying dividends fairly early on, and I captained the Haddonfield Memorial High School team that won the 1973 New Jersey state championship my senior year. It was a team that included some very hard-working, selfless players. We ended up going 28–2 and beating the highly regarded Orange High School team. Our coach, Dave Wiedeman, was not only a great coach, but he had more of a positive impact on my life than he will ever know. Looking back, I am certain he regularly used many of the words that are the focus of this book.

I feel comfortable saying that I was the hardest worker on the team. Whether I was the best player wasn't as important to me as being the hardest worker. I thought that *hardest worker* would be the greatest thing anyone could say about me, so I constantly pushed myself. When I was young, I knew other people ran to stay in shape. So, I wondered, how could I take that to another level? During the summers when we weren't in season, I ran. But I didn't just run like other people might; I checked the weather and then ran in the hottest part of the day. I would put on two pairs of sweats, two flannel shirts, add a weight jacket, a pair of ankle weights, and then another pair of sweats, then maybe one more flannel shirt. That's how I ran. I did it because when I met my competitors, I didn't want them to be able to say that they outworked me. No one would ever accuse me of not trying my hardest.

> *I believed that if I was the hardest worker, I would have a chance to become the best player I was capable of becoming.*

Off the court, I constantly read about NBA players and the best college players. As I read, I believed that if I was the hardest worker, I would have a chance to become the best player I was capable of becoming. I had long been a team-first player, but I always had that need, which I didn't recognize at the time, to do more, to do better, to be the best I could be.

My hard work paid off. From high school, I went to the University of Richmond on a basketball scholarship. My habits and mindset—maybe as much as my playing ability—helped me become a three-year starter and a captain. At the end of my senior season, the University created an award in my name. The Kevin Eastman Award has been given a handful of times since then to the player who exemplifies the combination of leadership, teamwork, and work ethic. In 2004 I was inducted into the UR Hall of Fame, an honor that meant as much as the one that took me back to my roots—induction into the HMHS Hall of Fame in 1990.

College was the end of my playing career, or so I thought. With the folding of the once-competitive American Basketball Association (ABA), another professional league was forming, the All American Basketball Alliance (AABA). This new league was based in Richmond. I was fortunate enough to make the team, but after four months (and no paychecks), the AABA folded. After this brief "professional" basketball experience—and still in love with the game—I decided to pursue coaching in the hope I might be able to help the next generation of players who shared the passion I felt for basketball.

If you were to ask me when I was in high school if I thought I would be a high school or college Hall of Fame player and then go on to coach major college basketball programs and an NBA World Championship team, I would have said, "No way." My vision never extended farther than what I was going to do tomorrow to make sure I could continue to do what I loved.

But I had this habit that stayed with me every day—the habit of trying.

Fast forward to June 2016 when I retired from coaching. After twenty-two years in college basketball (eleven years as a head coach and eleven years as an assistant coach), thirteen years in the NBA as an assistant coach with the Boston Celtics and Los Angeles Clippers, a year as Nike Basketball's director of skills academies, four years as a college athletic director, and a year as vice president of basketball operations with the Clippers, I was ready to practice coaching of a different sort. I wanted to share the words and wisdom I had learned along my way from working with the best of the best by speaking to corporate and sports teams.

Through those more than thirty-five years of coaching basketball, there were things I did, lessons I learned, concepts I perfected, and a mindset I developed that allowed me to have the success I have had in this game and in my life. I just didn't think about them at the time because I was too busy living them each day. In my mind, that was the only way I could become successful.

Stepping away from basketball allows me more time to pursue something I am passionate about and simply love doing. I'm sharing my observations about people and organizations, the lessons I've learned, and the incredibly fortunate experiences I've had. Looking back, I can see that the Power Words that are this book's focus were always part of my life; I just didn't always see them in that light.

I often say it's not about where you've been and what you've done, but about where you're capable of going and who you are capable of becoming. That has been my mindset, and that is what I will share with you in this book. If not for my mistakes, failures—and successes—I would not have a message worth sharing!

CHAPTER 1

I'm Standing in Front of The World Champions ...

I'm standing in front of the world champions ...
they just don't know it yet.

We've all seen it before. The picture of a coach standing in front of his team, sweat beading on his forehead, bags under his eyes from ten months on the uphill treadmill that is an NBA season.

But there's also an enormous smile of satisfaction and accomplishment on the coach's face. He stands before his team seeing his players' joy even though he knows their bodies are hurting, their lungs are empty, their legs are heavy from exertion. Together they have endured and triumphed in an emotional title game that has named his team the best in the world, the NBA World Champions.

We've all witnessed the triumphant locker room celebration, such an iconic moment of success, from the comfort of our living rooms.

> *I want to bring you with me to this place not many get to experience: inside an NBA locker room and inside the mindsets, habits, and strategies of champions.*

I spent my childhood wondering what it would be like to be inside that moment. I've been lucky. I have realized that moment. I have stood inside that locker room. In this book, I want to bring you with me to this place not many get to experience: inside an NBA locker room and inside the mindsets, habits, and strategies of champions.

But first, it isn't the champion's locker room I want to take you inside; that will come later. It's the locker room every player in the NBA walks into as each new season begins. And the only guarantee for anyone in this room is that there are no guarantees.

On this particular September day, the coach stood in front of his team long before a single game had been played. This locker room was in Waltham, MA, seventeen miles from the locker room the team uses when it plays its games at the new Boston Garden. This was the practice-facility locker room of the 2007/2008 Boston Celtics. Nine and a half months before one of the thirty NBA teams would be crowned the 2008 World Champions, Glenn "Doc" Rivers, the head coach of the Boston Celtics, stood before fifteen players seated in a "U" around him. They all wondered what teams would still be standing come June. Would they be among them and reach their goal of a championship?

The coaches and front office had made some bold, gutsy personnel changes during the off-season. How would this team mesh? Could they form a cohesive unit? All fifteen were waiting to hear what their coach would say. Would this be a tone-setting delivery that would have a lasting impact, or would it be just another coach pontificating a hope that would never materialize?

They all had seen and read what the media and fans had predicted during the off-season. With the addition of two of the best players in the game, Kevin Garnett and Ray Allen, and the return of NBA all-star Paul Pierce and future all-star Rajon Rondo, the buzz was that this group had "a chance" to be a "pretty good" team, but that they were not yet a lock as title contenders. We heard this—that we might be a year away from being a truly bona fide championship-caliber team—everywhere we turned. But one thing "everyone" forgot to do was tell Doc Rivers.

"I think we have enough in this locker room to win the title this year," were Doc's first words. This is a classic case of a statement that made a statement, the kind of message the best coaches send to their teams not just to create hope, but to set expec-

> *"I think we have enough in this locker room to win the title this year," were Doc's first words.*

tations. He believed this team could win a title. He wasn't just saying these words. I could see the belief in his eyes and hear it in the power of the words he spoke.

His words were met with silence. Heads snapped up in attention. The players' eyes drilled into Doc. It felt as if I could sense the pulse of their hearts pumping. Doc had the three most important things a leader could get from his team in that instant: their ears, their minds, and their hearts.

He continued. "In this room sits everything we need to win the title *this year!* It will be a season of good and bad, easy and hard, discussions and disagreements. But at the end of the day we have what we need to win it all THIS YEAR!

"BUT ... it will only work if you give yourselves up for the team. It will only work if you open yourselves up and allow me to coach you. But I am telling you, right here, right now—we have enough in this room to win it all THIS YEAR!"

This was September 29, 2007. On June 19, 2008, our team—the Boston Celtics—were crowned the 2008 NBA World Champions.

This group of trades, free agents, established players, and drafted players—this eclectic group of athletes—would go on to take the most important step there is to winning a championship. They would transform from simply a new group of athletes brought together in that Waltham locker room to the close-knit team pouring champagne on each other in the Boston Garden.

Message delivered? Goal accomplished? Easy?

Of course not! What was it about Doc's words that made them so powerful? What was the takeaway that we had to make sure we didn't give away?

One sentence. These were the simple, but powerful, words he spoke: "You have to give yourself up *to and for* the team."

That is what he said, but what he meant was even more impactful and harder to achieve. He meant: "You have to give yourselves up to **become** a team!"

They had to understand that: "We **need you** for what you can do … but only if you understand it cannot be **about you**."

That first sentence—just fifteen words, "I think we have enough inside this locker room to win the title this year"—set the tone and the standard for the journey this team was embarking on. That journey lasted ten months; 264 days; 116 games, ending with the 2008 Boston Celtics raising the world championship trophy.

SUCCESS IS MORE THAN THE CONFETTI AND TROPHIES

The impact of those fifteen words started the process of success for our team. And they started my thinking about the power of words and about the results carefully used words can produce. I started to reflect on my experiences over more than thirty-five years of coaching: the observations, conversations, debates, research, evaluations, and being in the fire on a daily basis. I became convinced that success comes down to the words people live by, the concepts they execute, and the understanding of the context around both.

Over my career, I have been a keen observer, listener, and thinker. I have honed my skills as a storyteller and simplifier of concepts as a coach and leader. I have put a great deal of thought into why people and teams progress, improve, and ultimately succeed. Why do some people and some teams outreach their perceived potential? Why do some overcome their lack of confidence? And to an even greater extent, why do teams win championships? Why do great leaders become great?

Working with the best of the best, I have found that there are certain words that every successful athlete, coach, employee, leader, team, and organization live by. These are words that are not simply in the vocabulary of high achievers, and—in my case—overachievers; they are words that guide their success journeys. I call these the Power Words of Champions.

What I will share with you in these pages are the words and concepts that I have gathered over a career of coaching in the NBA and NCAA. They are the words I live by. I define the words by the experiences I have been fortunate enough to have and by working closely with extraordinarily successful people. I have gathered the words you find in this book, along with some of the lists you will

> *I have gathered the words you find in this book, along with some of the lists you will encounter, over decades of thinking about success.*

encounter, over decades of thinking about success. I carry them with me and within me. If you were to look in my briefcase, you would find a blue folder. The folder is blue not just because that's my favorite color, but so that I can find it instantly. Within it you would find the lists I still consult daily. I might be stopped at a traffic light and slip it out of the briefcase. If I know I will be waiting for a meeting to start, the folder will already be in my hand, and because of the challenges I am facing that day you will find me opening that blue folder and consulting these words that have guided so much of my life. These lists allow me to:

- Turn lines into lessons.
- Turn red lights into reminders.
- Turn flights into classrooms.

I have learned that one man's wasted time is another man's learning time.

This book identifies and examines why these words produce the habits, mindsets, and results achieved by the most successful people in and out of sports. Words can simplify, provide direction, and create clarity. They teach us how to maximize our strengths, create new strengths, and reach our potential, guiding us to attain the goals we have set as adults and fulfill all the dreams we had as kids. When we momentarily lose direction, such words are a great reset mechanism to put us back on the path to success.

Many will say they have heard these words before—but they may not have lived them. They may think they are "old school," but as we define them for today's demands, we can change our use of them to "new-school" thinking. My mantra has been: "Old School— New School—ONE SCHOOL." That is the school of growth, development, and improvement. These are the words that have led to the success of many people we know as famous, but the magic of words is that they are available and free to all

> *My mantra has been: "Old School— New School—ONE SCHOOL." That is the school of growth, development, and improvement.*

of us. The difference is that some have chosen to insert them into their lives and not just have them in their vocabulary.

My experience as a coach has taught me that there is value in taking complex things and breaking them down into simple, understandable (and memorable) lessons. I believe that clarity and simplification are increasingly important in this demanding, cluttered, and ever-changing world. My philosophy throughout my adult life has been that *"success lies in simplicity; confusion lives in sophistication."* As Albert Einstein once said, "The definition of genius is taking the complex and making it simple." Those are the principles behind giving you these twenty-five proven and powerful words you can apply in your life.

Since becoming a speaker full time and traveling all over the world sharing ideas on leadership, culture, teamwork, how to have a repeat year, and how to become your best, I have been in many settings. I have been fortunate to speak in many locker rooms and also in many corporate boardrooms. While many may think there is a huge difference, I have actually seen an incredible consistency in those rooms. Sure, the locker rooms may be filled with taller and more athletic people, but both rooms have the same goals:

- To get the most out of their team.
- To get their team to be a team.
- To impact and inspire their team.
- To reach the goals they have set for their team.
- And most importantly—to win.

The biggest thing that we hope for in both rooms is that our people become the best they are capable of becoming. If they accomplish this, then we know we will get their best each and every day they enter our buildings. With everyone performing at their best, our team has the chance to perform at its best and to reach the goals we have set for that season or that fiscal year.

> *If we become a better version of ourselves, we have the chance to accomplish any goals, whether we're in a locker room or a boardroom.*

That was one of my motivations for writing this book: to help people become their best no matter what job they have, what field they're in, or what team they're working for. If we become a better version of ourselves, we have the chance to accomplish any goals, whether we're in a locker room or a boardroom.

Through this book I hope to provide you:

- **INFORMATION.** I will pass along new ideas or new ways to look at your personal success journey and how you can go farther and maybe even get there faster and better.

- **CONFIRMATION.** I will provide confirmation that some of the best of the best do things the way you are already doing them now and affirmation so you stop questioning yourself.

- **STIMULATION.** I will remind you that what you read may not hit you right away, but what I share can stimulate your thinking, so that when you are ready you can apply these concepts and make them yours.

What I will lay out for you in this book is the "how" to reach success. In particular, I will share

- the work that goes on behind success,
- the mindset that you can turn into a habit in order to succeed, and
- the execution discipline you can acquire to arrive at success.

Even as I pass along these words that have been my foundation, what's just as important is that you pick your own words to guide you in your search for success. This isn't a book you have to read in any particular order. If you are struggling with something in your life and you see a word that has relevance to you in that moment, jump ahead. I hope that by reading about the role such a word has had in the lives of extraordinarily successful people, you will find a way to apply it in your own life. You may view many of the athletes I use as examples in this book as having success beyond anything you can accomplish. But remember, the goal of this book is not to make you into a player in the NBA—it is to help you achieve the very best version of yourself. It's not about whether we can relate to the level they achieved, it's about making sure we learn the lessons of how they got there. Another thing worth remembering, which many don't realize, is that the majority of players in the NBA are role players, not stars. We all have roles to play. And this book is for people who want to play their roles to the very best of their ability.

We're all in different stages in life, as well, and I believe what I have laid out in this book will be able to touch most everyone. There are those who are looking for a *head start*, who are entering a profession and want to get up to speed a little faster. Others may need a *jump start* to reinvigorate them. Still others may need a *restart* after things may not have worked out for them. The ideas, strategies, and examples offered in this book can help everyone with their "start" right now—today—to get to where they always wanted to go in their job, career, and life!

> *It's not about what the words will do for you, it's all about what the words will do to you. That, to me, is their power. I can tell you from experience that if you apply these words and concepts, you will have a chance to become what you're capable of becoming.*

As you think about these words, keep in mind that it's not about what the words will do *for* you, it's all about what the words will do *to* you. That, to me, is their power. I can tell you from experience that if you apply these words and concepts, you will have a chance to become what you're capable of becoming. And the teams and organizations you're part of will be better for it, too. (This once shy, skinny Jersey boy is proof.)

My hope is that, by sharing what I've learned, I can have a small part in helping you in your job, career, performance, and life, so that you reach your adult-life goals and fulfill the dreams you had as a little kid! Thank you for letting me take you down this path of self-discovery and transformation.

24.

25. TALL

CHAPTER 2

The 25 Power Words of Champions

1. TRUTH

2. ACTION

3. INTENTIONAL

4. PREPARATION

5. ACCOUNTABILITY

6. TRUST

7. SACRIFICE

8. DISCIPLINE

9. COMMITMENT

10. BELIEF

11. UNREQUIRED

12. CHOICES

13. CIRCLES

14. COMPETITION

15. PASSION

16. HABITS

17. URGENCY

18. STANDARDS

19. COURAGE

20. CURIOSITY

21. RESPECT

22. ADJUSTMENT

23. HUMILITY

24. INVESTMENT

25. TALENT

So often today we fight the demands, the to-do lists, the time constraints, the pressure from our bosses, the projects at home, the clutter that fills our minds, and, of course, the everyday pressure to produce. The demands seem non-stop. They smother us and cause mental paralysis. We can never seem to catch up, let alone get ahead. Simply put, such demands trap us in a life of frustration, angst, and mental fatigue rather than one of daily concentration on how we can improve, grow, and love the life we are living.

I know (and knowing this has helped me throughout my life) that if I can simplify my thoughts, philosophies, and strategies, I will be able to call on them when I need them the most and get into execution mode without hesitation. For me, simplicity has kept hesitation, confusion, and doubt at bay and my mind clear. The core of the philosophies and strategies I live by can be captured in the Power Words that follow. These words become an action-able, memorable shorthand for powerful beliefs.

> *The core of the philosophies and strategies I live by can be captured in the Power Words that follow. These words become an actionable, memorable shorthand for powerful beliefs.*

able, memorable shorthand for powerful beliefs. As I suggested in chapter 1, not only do I *literally* carry these words with me every day, I have tried to gather the wisdom of others by paying close attention to how the best of the best approach their success journeys and their lives. They might all define these words with slight differences from how I have, but these words capture the mindsets that have helped them—and me—become successful.

As you digest these words, I challenge you to make them your own or to find other words that give you the personal meaning and motivation these have for me. And as you make these words, concepts, and ideas your own, I hope that along the way you find new and better ways of using them to be successful. What I'm certain of is that they will bring more clarity and efficiency to your life and to the challenges you face.

TRUTH

The average players want to be left alone.
The good players want to be coached.
The great players want to be told the truth.
**DOC RIVERS, NBA CHAMPIONSHIP COACH,
BOSTON CELTICS**

T here's an irony in the word *truth*. While truth can be something that is difficult to hear, it is also something that is critical to hear.

We are probably all looking for one word—and the complex concepts and beliefs a single word can express—that can transform our lives. Of course, we all know that such a single word does not exist, just as we know that success is never a single act but rather a combination of factors, experiences, and decisions. But if I were held to only one word that I believe is the most important for us to have ingrained in our everyday lives and thoughts, it would be the word *truth*.

My years in the NBA have taught me a very important lesson about success at the highest levels: the NBA is a "truth league." Becoming successful in our lives or careers is always about the truth. Neither the league I was in nor the success we all wish to achieve can withstand the destructive power of lies. In the NBA and in life, the truth will ultimately be revealed. You will be exposed for what you are not. The truth will tell you whether you belong or not. It is the one word that all great athletes, coaches, and leaders demand to be told.

Truth needs three things:

- You must be able to live it.
- You must be able to tell it.
- You must be able to take it.

LIVE IT

We all know those people who talk a good game and produce nothing in the end. How many colleagues or teammates have you had in your life who say they are going to change their habits—and two months later you find they have not changed?

Doc Rivers always started training camp with a dinner that included the team and coaching staff the night before the first practice. At this dinner, Doc set the tone for the year. Often he would ask for input from the players. One year he asked a player what he wanted to prove to people that year. The player's response was immediate; he said he wanted to "let people know that I'm not the player they say I am." Everyone in the room knew his reputation as being lazy defensively, having poor shot selection, and not always being a team-first guy. We were all hopeful when he said he was going to change. Two months into the season, however, he was playing exactly as he always had in the past. In my book, that player was not living his truth.

The old adage states that we must "put our money where our mouth is." When we are talking about living the truth, I have always said that we must "match the actions we take with the words we speak." Clearly, this player was not matching his actions on the court with his words at that dinner.

The ultimate outcome was that we had to get rid of him. Was this a harsh action for us to take? Maybe. Was it action that was needed for team success? Definitely! You see, when it comes to decisions about your team, you must make those decisions through the lens of what is best for the team, not necessarily what is best for the individual. In the case of becoming a championship-level team, you have to have team members who "live the truth."

TELL IT

There are two truths that exist: the truth that people love to hear—and the truth that they do not want to hear. As leaders, coaches, and teammates, we want to make sure that we deliver both when they need delivering. But we all know that the hard truths are called that for a reason; they are hard to hear and equally hard to tell.

When I was the VP for basketball operations for the Los Angeles Clippers, I found out early that hard conversations were a required part of sitting in a leadership seat and that hard truths needed to be told if I truly was looking out for the best interests of the organization and of the people reporting to me. These hard truths and hard conversations revolved around situations that happen in all industries, like those times when you have to put someone on notice for lack of production or fire someone because he or she is not meeting the expectations of the position. Neither is easy, but both are necessary if we are doing our best for the betterment of the organization or trying to create a culture focused on success.

Telling such truths was hard for me. I simply do not like to make people feel bad if I can help it. However, being a leader requires us to do the uncomfortable thing in certain situations. Realizing that telling people hard truths was part of the position, I decided immediately that I needed a strategy that allowed me to do my job while also allowing the person receiving the tough news the respect and dignity he or she deserved.

This was my framework:

- Be direct and to the point.
- Always speak the facts and the truth.
- Speak with respect and empathy.
- Allow them to vent.

I think you can see the importance of the first three, but when I speak to leadership teams around the country and we talk about these challenging parts of leadership, they often ask, "Why the fourth one? I don't want to hear them vent." Part of leadership is doing what is best for those we lead. Letting them vent was often best for certain people. My hope was that they could take some of their frustration out on me and not on whomever crossed their path once they left my office. I always reminded myself that they had to tell their spouse, their children, and their friends that they were no longer of value to our organization. That is not an easy message to live with if you have any level of pride.

This framework allowed me to keep the emotion out of these "tell-it" meetings. We all have been in meetings where emotion ruled, and they almost never turn out to be productive.

I often reference a thought that I heard from Jerry West, an NBA Hall of Famer. When he was the general manager of the Los Angeles Lakers, he told me that he "put a lot of pre-thought to hard decisions and difficult conversations." These are simple words laced with wisdom. They are words I applied in those tough situations where I had to "tell it." Think about the message you want to send and how you want to send it. Then think about the response you may get.

TAKE IT

Hearing the truth is not always pleasant. Often it delivers a message of what we are not doing, what we need to do better, where we were deficient, or how we are hurting our team. While this is difficult, it is also necessary if we truly want to reach our goals. It is imperative that we hear the truth, because it is crucial that we know what we need to do, what we need to improve, and what we need to learn in order to get to where we want to go.

We've all heard the expression that "the truth hurts." I do not believe this at all—provided you have the right mindset. The truth may make your ears red with embarrassment, but the truth actually helps, not hurts. That is the mindset that all the great ones live by.

The other age-old saying is that "the truth will set you free." I agree with this, but when it comes to being your best self or your best team, you have to look at truth in a different light. Whereas the truth may set you free, the best of the best will tell you that the truth will actually "set you up." It will set you up for your development. It will set you up for your growth. It will set you up for your improvement. Truth is the key ingredient to success that tells you exactly what you need to do, what you need to change, and what you need to improve upon.

I have had the good fortune of coaching or working with many of basketball's greatest players like Kevin Garnett, Lebron James, Kevin Durant, Paul Pierce, Ray Allen, and many others. One thing stands true for them all: they demanded the truth from their coaches and teammates.

When Kevin Garnett first joined the Celtics, he met with Doc Rivers and asked Doc to tell him the truth if he was going to be his best and the team was going to be its best. There could be no half-truths or sugar coating—because success has no room for either.

I am reminded of Kevin when I think back to working with a

young Lebron James before the draft in 2003. Nike called to see if I would be willing to come out to their Beaverton, OR campus as they were meeting with Lebron to pitch him on joining the Nike family of endorsers. Nike believes in the total person and not just whether they wear the shoe. They wanted a part of Lebron's visit to include a workout. I met Lebron in Nike's campus gym. I was told to give him a forty-five-minute workout. What ensued became more than that. It became a lesson in the best wanting to hear the truth.

We were about seven minutes into game-speed shooting, except there was only one person going game speed—me. Lebron was still moving at what I told him was "high school" speed. I wondered if I was pushing too hard too soon as he had just finished his senior year in high school and this was the first time we ever met. But he was about to enter a level completely different from any he had ever experienced. I kept on him about going game speed and being intentional about the fundamentals. I pushed him hard, maybe even sprinkling in a word or two that would not be said in church.

About seventy-five minutes later, both of us were drenched with sweat. I wanted to make sure he knew I was pushing him "for" him. I said, "Hey, I didn't mean to come down that hard on you." I will never forget his answer. "I'm good. I want to know everything I need to know to get better." For many who are reading this, his response may just roll off the page, never to be thought about again. However, those who really want to succeed, have to see the lessons that were in Lebron's statement. As Doc Rivers said with frequency: "I know what he said—but what did he *say?*"

What Lebron *said* was that he wanted to hear the truth about the next level. He needed the truth to get to where he wanted to go. He didn't care if it hurt; he understood how it would help!

I could have missed what else was contained in his words had I not thought back on that day. He said he wanted to know "everything I need to know to get better." What he taught me that day is the secret to success. Becoming our best is not a one-time step we take, it's a process we go through. He taught me, without knowing it, that there's a formula for success: *Better + Better + Better + Better = Best.*

It may take more days of getting better for some people than others, and that's okay. Just stick with getting better each day without worrying about being the best. What I have learned from studying the journeys of successful people is that it takes a lot of years to become an overnight sensation.

THE TRUTH "MUSTS"

Finally, let me ask you to consider doing three things:

- **Have a "truth teller" in your inner circle**, as George Raveling always professed. (We have all heard this, but it's important to repeat.) You have to hear what you *need* to hear, not what you *want* to hear. There are a lot of unsuccessful people who have never wanted to hear the truth; they've also never tasted the success they dreamed of having!

- **Conduct a "truth audit" at least once a year.** Sit down with yourself and evaluate where you are relative to where you want to be, and list those things that are keeping you from getting there. This is not an easy assignment, but it is one that has really helped me. The one person who should know me the best is myself. There is a lot of con in this world, but the one person you can never con is yourself.

- **Act on what you hear.** Change what you need to change. Learn what you need to learn. And if you don't know how to do that, find people who can help you. The information you will receive from completing the first two "musts" is only going to be useful if you act on it.

The best are the best for a reason, and one of the reasons is that they live in the world of the truth. They are willing to—and, in fact, demand—to be told the truth. And they understand the most important truth is the "truth in the mirror." When we look in the mirror, the person we see knows the entire truth. Those who succeed are the ones who hear what the mirror says and act on the things it tells us that need work!

ACTION

You get better by doing.
You don't get better by talking about doing.
CARL LIEBERT, EXECUTIVE VP AND COO, USAA

I think we all would agree that no matter how many ideas you have and how many goals you've set, they all just sit in your head until you decide to take action. And I would argue that when you fail to take action on such ideas, they don't just sit in your head, they mess with your head. They pile up on top of one another, and as you focus on the actions you have *not* taken, they create frustration and regret. When I had the privilege of working as a consultant for Nike, their corporate motto—Just Do It!—was more than an ad campaign for me. It was a daily reminder to take action!

One of the highlights of my life was an experience with a team of military pararescue leaders in Alaska. I was asked to speak to the leadership team of the 212th Rescue Squadron at a retreat a few hours into the mountains outside Anchorage. I knew going there that I would also have an opportunity to learn from them. After all, these are people who live in the world of special operations and go directly into harm's way to save lives and transport wounded soldiers for treatment. Sometimes the mission is to retrieve a body to return to the soldier's family for proper burial.

The first day with them, I could tell they were trying to figure out who this NBA guy was and what he might bring to the table. Not knowing anyone, I did what I always do in those situations, I asked questions. The burning questions I had were: "What makes you guys do what you do each time out? How can you do it knowing you may not come back alive?"

Their answers were simple, yet profound, and have everything to do with action. They said three things that will be etched in my mind forever:

> *The burning questions I had were: "What makes you guys do what you do each time out? How can you do it knowing you may not come back alive?"*

- **Our motto is "That Others May Live."** It's not that *they* may live when they go on a mission into dangerous situations, it's so "that *others* may live." They take action for others.

- **"We try."** They were saying, "Sure these are very dangerous missions that could have bad results but at the very least, we must try. We owe that to their families and to those soldiers who need our help."

- **"We don't quit."** Everybody thinks of the word action as just that first effort to start, but it's more than that for these special ops forces. They can't and they won't quit. Their mission is too important. There's too much on the line. If it's important to try, it sure as hell is important enough not to quit.

> *If it's important enough to try, it sure as hell is important enough not to quit.*

My takeaway was that so much of what makes them who they are is that they start at the start: They try. They take action. They often don't know the exact environment they are going into; they don't know what the enemy may have in store; they don't even know if the mission will be successful. But they at least try. They take action. You can imagine how immediately I was brought to attention by their use of the word "try," a concept that is at the center of who I am.

The second thing I learned is if it's important enough for us to try something, we have to make sure it remains important enough not to quit. Don't let your effort be determined by success or failure, by win or loss. Let the determining factor be the personal importance of it, the purpose that made you try in the first place.

Remember that success is smart. It will test us at many turns. And its biggest test is failure. It wants to know if you will quit. That's why a central theme of the talks I give around the country to business and sports teams includes:

- Failure is part of all successful team and individual journeys.

- You cannot fear failure; it happens to the best of the best.

- If you fear the consequence of failure, put equal fear to the consequence of never trying. What would happen if you tried, and *it worked!* Imagine if you knew you would succeed, but you didn't try. How would you feel then?

Although our lives and decisions may not rise to the level of life-and-death importance as the 212th Rescue Squadron, let's still take their lessons to heart. What if our philosophy was simply: Try, and don't quit. Act, and don't quit.

My guess is that we would all feel a lot better about ourselves as we accomplished more than we thought we could. This philosophy is a great formula for all of us to reach our potential.

So often we know what to do, but we fail to do what we know. When action becomes a core ingredient of who you are, you will consistently do what you know should be done. Action is incredibly powerful ... provided you take it!

> *When action becomes a core ingredient of who you are, you will consistently do what you know should be done. Action is incredibly powerful ... provided you take it!*

INTENTIONAL

It's not about what you want.
It's about what you do every day.

BRAD STEVENS, HEAD COACH, BOSTON CELTICS

Two great questions to gauge where you are on your journey of growth are:

1. Do you truly want to grow, develop, and improve?

2. What are you *intentionally* doing *every day* to make sure you do?

This I know for sure: sustained success is not an accident. It is a combination of thoughtful, intentional actions and strategies. Success is a result of what we purposefully do, not what we accidently fall into.

I found that when I added the word *intentional* to my success vocabulary and tried to live it each day, my growth seemed to evolve naturally. The key is that intentional is a daily action. It takes pinpoint thinking and serious planning. It's not a "maybe on Wednesday" or "I'll get to it on Monday." It's an everyday mindset. These are actions you take because you've determined they can help

> *When I added the word intentional to my success vocabulary and tried to live it each day, my growth seemed to evolve naturally.*

you arrive where you want to be in your career, become who you have always dreamed of becoming in your life, and achieve the growth you will need to accomplish both.

A word of caution here: there is a huge difference between *intention* and *intentional*. I know people who have great intentions to do great things with their lives, but they never get around to them. They have not turned intention into an intentional act. Intentional is all about keeping it front of mind and first to action. This is at the core of living an intentional life.

I can tell you that once I made reading an intentional part of my life, I not only gained more knowledge, but also more confidence. I made it an intentional daily act to read two hours every day, seven days a week without exception. Now I know you might say, "How can I find two hours every day to read? I don't even have enough time to keep up with my life." My answer is respectful yet simple as I always pose a question back: "How can I *not* find that time?"

If I want to grow, if I want to improve, if I want to develop, if I want to stay relevant, if I want to keep up with the best practices of others at levels I aspire to, how could I not find ways to accomplish these goals? I had to make reading an intentional part of my life. I am proud to say in the years since making that decision, I have read at least two hours on well over ninety-five percent of those days. Being intentional provides a focus on what we believe is most important.

Intentional turns a to-do list to a must-do list!

PREPARATION

Prepare for the future because that is where
you are going to spend the rest of your life.

MARK TWAIN, AUTHOR

How many times have we gone into a sales pitch, a meeting, a public speech, or a game and wished we had prepared a little more? Done one more thing. Rehearsed one more time. Showed our team one more way to defend our opponent. The same holds true for the best of the best in the world. They also have to prepare each and every day, but they have risen to be the best because they put preparation so high on their "must-do" list.

They understand that the knowledge and confidence they get from preparation is a separator. Preparation creates knowledge, and knowledge breeds confidence. They understand that preparation allows them to be ready for the unexpected because they know knowledge is quickness. And quickness to recognize and react is often the difference between winning and losing, whether that is on the court, in the sales meeting, or within the boardroom.

The best of the best separate themselves by their preparation. So let me give you my definition of the word:

BE THERE BEFORE YOU GET THERE.

What if every one of us always prepared with this in mind? Be there before you have to give that big presentation. Be there before you have to pitch that big client. Be there before you have to take and make that last-second shot.

Let me set the stage: NBA finals 2013. Miami Arena. Miami is down 2–3 in the series and trailing by three with eleven seconds left. Lebron James takes a three-point shot from the top of the floor right in front of the Miami Heat bench. The shot caroms off the rim and Chris Bosh gets a critical offensive rebound. Ray Allen sees Bosh is going to get it and has the presence of mind to start back pedaling to the right corner behind the three-point line. He never has to waste a second by looking down to see if he is behind the line. Bosh kicks the ball out to Ray, and Ray shoots the three; swish. Miami wins game six. It was "the shot" that won the title for the Heat that year as they went on to win game seven and the NBA championship.

I am often asked about that shot because people know I worked with Ray and witnessed the practice he put in every day while I assisted Doc Rivers in Boston. I don't know how many people said to me, "What a lucky shot that was." Such a reaction could not be further from the truth. Ray had already been there thousands of times before in his practice workouts. He had taken that exact same shot over and over and over again. He knew what that moment would be like because he had prepared for it.

He understood the three things preparation can do for you:
- Preparation trumps pressure.
- Preparation fuels confidence.
- Preparation becomes your separation.

I would be remiss if I did not speak to the importance of the *depth* of preparation that is needed. The Iceberg Principle comes into play here, the phenomenon we are all familiar with that only about ten percent of an iceberg's mass is visible above the water. The strength of the iceberg is underneath the surface, unseen. Preparation is the unseen grind that produces the biggest plays under the brightest lights. Like an iceberg, the *depth* of your preparation is where your strength will come as you tackle challenges.

> *Preparation is the unseen grind that produces the biggest plays under the brightest lights.*

I had the good fortune to discuss the value of preparation with Erik Logan, who is president of the Oprah Winfrey Network. Erik is a deep thinker and is filled with wisdom. When I asked him his thoughts on preparation he said, "I spend one hour preparing for every ten minutes I will be speaking."

It made immediate sense that preparation is a major part of why Erik is so successful. He understands the work that shows itself under the lights is only able to happen because of the preparation he does when the lights aren't on and no one is watching. As Erik modestly told me, preparation is what allowed him to climb the ladder even though he considers himself the consummate underdog!

THE QUESTION BECOMES: HOW DEEP DO WE TAKE OUR PREPARATION?

We will all be in difficult situations. We will all face pressure. We will all have some level of doubt at times. That is where preparation is most useful. That is where the right preparation is most powerful. The key to success is making sure that your preparation is greater than any challenge, issue, or problem you will face.

Ray Allen made sure he was there before he got there, practicing his shot every day—even on the game days when most players were trying to conserve energy. I would often meet Ray in the hotel lobby with some of our other assistant coaches early enough so that Ray could make sure he was at the arena three hours before the game. From the moment we entered a cab on our way to the arena, we were in total game-preparation mode.

Once at the arena, Ray would go through his thirty-minute routine with the intensity he would need once he was in real game action. This was practice, yes, but he was practicing game shots from game spots at game speed. He wanted to make sure that what he felt in the practice shooting he would go on to feel in the game, from the cut to the catch to the jump off the floor to the silky-smooth touch of his shot.

One drill caught me off guard before an early season game. Ray was about halfway through his routine when I turned back to pass to him after rebounding his shot—to find him on his stomach doing push-ups, which caused his arms to tighten up. Anyone watching would assume he was losing his mind. He wasn't. He was Ray being brilliant.

The drill called for him to jump up from his prone position and spring to a spot on the floor where we would pass to him and he would shoot. Teams always guarded Ray physically, which caused him to use his strength to break away and get open. This exertion of strength caused his arms to tighten up, just as the push-ups did. No shooter wants tightness in his arms when he shoots. Ray's brilliance was in his preparation; it simulated exactly how he would feel in the game. Ray's depth of preparation was his separator.

Ray understands, and you must too, how to: *be there before you get there!*

ACCOUNTABILITY

If there's any question as to who should
take the blame, I take the blame.

DWANE CASEY, HEAD COACH, DETROIT PISTONS
2018 NBA COACHES ASSOCIATION COACH OF THE YEAR

If winning is important, accountability is a must! If success is the goal, accountability is a must. If fulfilling your dreams is your hope, accountability is a must. The winner's mindset is: "I will hold myself accountable." It's the ultimate "look inside first" action anyone can take. Accountability is a personal commitment to deliberately take ownership of your actions. This is the mentality that allows teams and individuals to become their best.

> *Accountability is a personal commitment to deliberately take ownership of your actions. This is the mentality that allows teams and individuals to become their best.*

Success demands accountability and accountability demands ownership and truth. Accountability is taking ownership of all that you do and all that you say, regardless of the ramifications. Accountability is an "inward-first" evaluation where you look at your part in the loss or the failure. No loss I have ever been involved in ever came down to one individual or one play. Everyone could have done something better, from coaches to players. Accountability has to fall on everyone every day if goals are to be met and potential is to turn into production.

Let's look at the opposite type of team: the teams of blame, of victims, of lies. Whereas success demands accountability, and accountability requires us to look within ourselves, failure encourages us to look outward first. To blame first. *It had to be someone else's fault.* Losing teams look to blame someone else so that they can portray themselves as the victims. They play the victim and look for sympathy rather than looking inward and finding solutions.

On teams Doc Rivers coached, we talked about never allowing yourself to *be* the victim, never allowing yourself to *play* the victim. In a competitive environment, victims never succeed and blame teams never win. Blame leads to resentment. Resentment leads to dislike. Dislike leads to disharmony. And ultimately all of these lead to a breakdown in the essential ingredient to team success: trust. If you don't own up to your actions and responsibilities, how can anyone trust you?

My experience competing at the highest levels has shown me that there are decisions to make when it comes to accountability. You can choose to be:

- A team of accountability or a team of blame.
- A player of accountability or a player of blame.
- A leader of accountability or a leader of blame.
- A person of accountability or a person of blame.

You can see where I am going with this list. These are the decisions we have to apply to any job we hold, team we're on, or goal we have. What I can tell you for a fact is that if you want to produce at a championship level, accountability has to be a staple of operation.

Accountability is a major ingredient of winning. Winning teams are always keenly aware of who they must be accountable *to* and what they must be accountable *for*. These championship-level teams understand they are accountable

- to their teammates;
- for themselves, their role, and their improvement;
- to the organization;
- for the results (both good and bad); and
- for carrying out and policing a culture of accountability.

An accountability culture has to start at the top from both the leaders of the team and the best players on the team. The best way to create the buy-in to an accountability-driven team is for them to educate and exemplify that accountability is mandatory. They must also instill a mindset that says accountability doesn't just mean admitting mistakes and failures as much as it shows us what to work on, and that drives success. It provides a starting point for where we need to go next and what we need to do better. It is a positive force for improvement, not a continuous admittance of failure. This distinction is huge if people are going to buy into being accountable!

Paul Gartlan, president and CEO of Skybox, Inc., an international e-commerce logistics company, feels accountability is everything in his small business. Like many, he does not have the resources to hire unlimited managers to oversee everything while he sits in his office with his feet on the desk. His company's success depends on Paul hiring the employees with the character he wants in order to have the accountability he needs.

He has known the importance of accountability since his basketball-playing days at Randolph-Macon College and ten years playing professionally in Chile. He believes, "In the business world, accountability is everything because, for the most part, our team spends most time working when no one else is watching." The charge he gives to those in his company is to "think like an owner. Think and work like you are paying the bills. If you apply that mentality in everything you do for the company, it is impossible not to be a tremendous asset to the company."

Where the best workers separate themselves is in adhering to this "ownership mentality" that Paul talks about, combined with the adherence to personally high standards. As I will discuss a little later in the book, one form of competition that the best of the best is well aware of is *competing against yourself.* A major part of personal competition is holding yourself accountable each and every day to the high standards the organization has set for its team and the even higher standards you have set for yourself.

In my years with the Celtics, I don't know how many times after a loss Doc would say to the media (and for all to hear) "This loss is on me." Or "It's my job to prepare my team, and I did not do that well enough tonight." He was willing to own up not just to the public but to our team that he has to keep improving just as he demands that the team improve. He was strong enough in his belief in himself that he was willing to admit his mistakes and failures. From a leadership point of view, our guys felt he was right there in it with them because he took ownership. When a team feels the coach is in it with them, there is no telling what they will do for that coach!

I can also cite many times when future Hall of Famer Kevin Garnett would be the first to speak in the locker room after a loss—and he would put the loss squarely on his own shoulders. But his team also knew with Kevin that whatever mistakes he accepted responsibility for would not happen again. Kevin kept his mistakes in his memory bank and used them as motivational challenges.

So, I guess you get the point that I strongly believe in the word accountability. But I have to tell you it is not the only *"bility"* that is important! I know what you're thinking, so let me address it before we go any farther. Yes, *"bility"* is a word … in *my* dictionary. Maybe not in Webster's but it is in mine.

MASTER THE BILITIES

As you look at this list, you will see key words all champions live by. Most importantly, as you read these "bilities", think about this: "What if everyone in our organization mastered and lived these words every day? What if they held themselves to the highest standards these words embody? Where would our organization be then? How high could our team go?

- **Responsibility.** Do your job completely.

- **Accountability.** Take ownership of your words, actions, decisions, mistakes, and failures.

- **Dependability.** Can we count on you?

- **Vulnerability.** You don't always have to be right; we just need to get it right.

- **Adaptability.** Can you change and adjust as needed?

- **Credibility.** Do your actions match your words? Are you competent? Do you demonstrate integrity?

- **Compatibility.** Do you value teamwork? Do you understand what it takes to be a great teammate?

- **Availability.** Do you bring all that you have every day? Are you there and prepared to go every day?

- **Stability.** Can you compete with composure? Can you play with emotion but not get emotional?

- **Capability.** Can you reach your maximum potential when we need it most?

- **Sustainability.** Can you deliver every day or are you a "one-hit wonder"?

Like accountability, championship teams and organizations are built on these words. Such teams have the "bility" to live by these words every day. These words travel home or away!

How important do I think these words are to success? Important enough that in my very first meeting I had as vice president of basketball operations with the Los Angeles Clippers I handed this list out to every person who reported to me. I wanted them to let these words soak in and then put thought to how much better they would be if they tried to master these "bilities" every day they came to work and in all parts of their lives. And then I asked them to think about how much better our organization would be if we mastered and lived these words and their definitions each day.

TRUST

It's at the core of what we do and who
we are. It allows you to navigate through
the challenging times of the year.

**CHERYL REEVE, HEAD COACH, MINNESOTA LYNX
FOUR-TIME WNBA CHAMPION**

Arguably the one word we hear more than almost any other when it comes to team dynamics is *trust*. This is true for good reason: trust is critical in any endeavor where groups of people are working together. There has to be an unwritten understanding that everyone will do their job to the best of their ability every time, every day. There has to be comfort knowing that when help is needed, help will be there, whether that is on the football field where the quarterback knows that the linemen will work to give him enough time to find an open receiver or in the office where a salesperson must trust that his coworkers will make sure the right product will be shipped to the right address at the right time. There must be trust that each person will do his or her job so that everyone else can do their job.

I define trust in the context of time, knowing full well that in today's world everything has to be completed *now*. Trust does not work on the clock. Trust, in fact, needs three things to be strong, with its most important requirement being that it will never allow itself to be rushed. Trust needs:

- time,
- consistency, and
- proof.

No one is going to trust anyone else immediately; it takes time to see how that person operates and to experience his or her intentions. Trust is built through the accumulation of words and actions, but most importantly, it's not the words you speak, it's the actions you take and the intention behind these actions that creates true trust.

Trust needs consistency. Can I count on you every time? Do you bring energy and effort every day or only on days when you feel like it? Do you talk one way when

> *Trust needs consistency.*

I'm in front of you and the opposite when I'm not around? When I ask myself if I can trust you, your consistency will play a big part in my decision.

And finally, trust needs proof. If you say you are going to do something, do it! If you say you are going to be somewhere, get there! If you promise something, deliver it!

One of the best examples I've heard about trust came from Ross Comerford, CEO of Fast Model, when he said: "I know we have a culture of trust when we don't have to erase the whiteboards!" Trust is built upon action over weeks, months, and years, but it can be destroyed in seconds. Give yourself the time to build it, but make sure you don't stop there. Trust isn't just a building project, it's every bit a maintenance project as well.

SACRIFICE

I like to call them deposits because when you're
passionate about what you want to do, it doesn't
feel like you're giving anything up.

**BETH MOWINS, PLAY-BY-PLAY ANNOUNCER,
ESPN AND CBS**

T he 2008 Boston Celtics championship team allowed
me to see what sacrifice was up close and personal on
an everyday basis. I want to make sure I overemphasize
"everyday" because convenient sacrifice is not true
sacrifice. There are certain things that success declares we do every
day. One of them is sacrifice. There is no expiration date on sacrifice
if individuals or a team wants to reach their true capability level.

> *Convenient sacrifice*
> *never wins; it is*
> *actually selfishness*
> *disguised.*

Convenient sacrifice never wins;
it is actually selfishness disguised. The
individual looks like he is sacrificing,
but upon closer look, he allows others
to receive some acknowledgement or
minor notoriety only after receiving
his own accolades. A player may sacrifice something insignificant,
like one shot on one possession, or one interview with the small-town
paper, or one small bit of revenue for a teammate—but when it comes
time to sacrificing more prestigious opportunities in favor of the organization, sacrifice suddenly becomes secondary to the "convenient

sacrificer." Teams with people like this are operating on false success. They will never be as good as they are capable of being.

Sacrifice is giving up something that you may really want for something bigger that may or may not happen in the future. Or as Doc Rivers likes to say, "Doing something that may not be good for you but is better for the team." In other words, sacrifice becomes a decision to go against the pull of human nature to look out for oneself.

The 2008 Boston Celtics offered many examples of sacrifice that began before the very first game that year. Kevin Garnett, the ultimate sacrifice player, shot down the popular notion that, with his arrival, the Celtics would now become "his team." Kevin made sure that people knew the Celtics were still Paul Pierce's team. Kevin believes that you earn status because of the work and sacrifice you have put in, and he knew Paul had done so for all the years he had been in Boston. How many people would have given up all the attention that would have gone with the image of the Celtics being "their team?" Kevin sacrificed what may have been good for him for what he knew was best for the team and what he knew was right for Paul Pierce.

That year, the Big Three, as they were known—Paul Pierce, Kevin Garnett, and Ray Allen—all took fewer shots per game than their game averages over their past years. For players who had long been counted on to score, players designated by former teams as "shot takers," fulfilling a different role is a huge sacrifice. And it proved to be the right choice! We went 66–16, the best record in the NBA, on the way to winning the championship. They understood that teams win championships, not individuals, and true teams require true sacrifices.

There are two ways to look at sacrifice:

- As the act of giving something up.

  OR

- The opportunity to help something more.

The 2008 Boston Celtics saw sacrifice as helping one another more. As a result, all three marquee players, and all of their teammates, ended the season lifting the world championship trophy!

DISCIPLINE

Discipline lives at the door of decisions because
saying yes means saying no to another.
Remembering what you want drives those decisions.

**SHERRI COALE, HEAD COACH,
UNIVERSITY OF OKLAHOMA**

A s a young coach, I always went to as many coaching clinics as I could find and afford, as they provided opportunities to learn from some of the best coaches in the game. There are times for all of us when wisdom walks into our lives and impacts us by a simple sentence someone spoke or a simple action we observed. It happens often to me, as I am a huge believer in keeping my learning antennas up at all times. If wisdom is coming my way, I want to be ready to capture it.

At the podium of a clinic I attended in Cherry Hill, New Jersey stood Bobby Knight, who was then the coach at Indiana. Coach Knight was regarded as one of the best (if not the best) coaches of all time. When he spoke, you listened. He defined discipline as, "Doing what needs to be done when it needs to be done as well as it can be done and doing it that way all the time." I thought this was one of the best definitions of discipline, and I have kept it as my foundation of what discipline is and how I should go about exercising it.

I encourage everyone to look at discipline as the tool we need to get us through the days when we don't feel like doing the very thing

> *I encourage everyone to look at discipline as the tool we need to get us through the days when we don't feel like doing the very thing we know has been a key ingredient to our success.*

we know has been a key ingredient to our success. We all have those days where we just don't seem to have the mindset, the energy, or the will to remain disciplined. Such days are simply a test that success often throws in front of us. Will you do what you know is leading to your success on this day at this time when you simply do not feel like doing it?

Success doesn't wait for anyone. It requires many, many discipline decisions, also known as success decisions. This situation I have described is one of them: are you disciplined enough to do the work on the days you don't feel up to it?

The great ones do. And one of the most important disciplines they have is their daily routine. They have a practice routine. They have a game day routine. They have a sleep routine. They eat at the same time on game day. They read at the same time. Routine is the daily discipline that is needed for success. The discipline is the inner push that serves as the reminder to get the routine done.

For Ray Allen, as we have seen, it was being on the court taking his game-day shots in the arena three hours before game time. Not two hours and fifty-five minutes. Not three hours and twelve minutes. Silly? No! Smart? Yes, as proven by his all-star career and his induction into the Hall of Fame.

On game day, Ray had a set time to eat, to nap, and to shower. All purposely scheduled so he would be in the arena dressed and ready to shoot three hours before game time. This disciplined routine is what made Ray Allen Ray Allen. He understood that discipline is critical for success. He also understood that discipline allowed him to overcome the temptations to which the average players fall victim, to overcome living in the world of "what's easiest for me." Discipline says no to easy and says yes to whatever it needs to do to succeed and fulfill one's capabilities.

COMMITMENT

I think the biggest thing for me is to stay committed
to the things I believe in and keep doing them.

QUIN SNYDER, HEAD COACH, UTAH JAZZ

I will often ask players what time zone they operate in most often. When I pose this question, I get some weird looks, because they automatically think of the time zones across the country. But the time zones I am talking about are the time zones of success. These are the times zones of winners vs. losers. The time zones I am referring to are:

- **Spare time**: I'll do it when I get to it.
- **Part time**: I'll do it every now and then.
- **Full time:** I'll do it when and only when it's required, but I will do it.
- **All the time:** I will do what it takes, and more, every time you need me regardless of the circumstances.

As you look at this list, think about which ones produce winning and which ones create frustration and contribute to losing. There is no doubt that if you are part of a team of "spare-time" and "part-time" people, you have no shot at reaching your goals. You just never know when these two types of people will show up. And if you have to guess each day what time zone your colleagues or teammates are in, there's simply no way the group can succeed. Success is all about consistency.

If you have "full timers" on your team, you at least have a shot, because they will attempt to do what is required, though even that may not be enough. Most every team that goes far does the required work, but championship teams not only do the required work; they separate themselves from others by doing the unrequired work. Good workers do the required work of their job description. "Champion" workers represent the "all-the-time" players and are the ones who are consistently willing to do that unrequired work. They put in the extra reps, study the scouting report one more time, help a struggling teammate after practice. They define commitment.

Commitment has no expiration date. Commitment is an every day, every week, every month, every year proposition. You're either in or you're not. There is no such thing as being committed on Monday but not on Friday.

A great example of commitment is Tracy Mazzoni. Tracy began her career at Merrill Lynch, working her way up from new employee to earning the position of managing director, head of client management, Merrill Edge. Managing director is a highly respected position that is difficult to achieve in the financial-services industry. It took a strong commitment to reach.

I met Tracy the first time I spoke to a group of Merrill Lynch financial advisors. In one of those sessions Tracy shared her story about growing up in a trailer in a small country town and about being diagnosed with multiple sclerosis as a young adult. Where she grew up, she explained, people seldom spoke about the future, retirement, or financial planning, yet she was determined to enter the business and climb the success ladder. Once in the industry, she set a goal to become a managing director.

When I asked her about the drive inside of her, she talked about commitment being key. It took her sixteen years to earn her way up the ladder—and she was driven by this commitment. She explains that we all "start out fresh, pumped up, sky is the limit on what you can do, but then we get caught up in the middle; the weeks, months, and years where you are doing the same things all the time day in and day out. It's a very mundane and not too glamorous time of your career."

Tracy fought through this middle and reached her goal, but her commitment didn't stop. She told me she doesn't want to fall into the trap that sometimes catches people who have worked a long time to reach a certain level in their careers. She said she doesn't want to "lean on her title." She also adds: "You have to bring your best self to work and show up every day like you are on a job interview and everyone is watching. Everyone knows where the talent is regardless of where you are in the organization. There is always an opportunity to get your name on a short list even when you don't know a short list exists."

> Commitment has to be a resolve to fight through difficulties when others around you are criticizing you, when teammates are doubting you, or when your goal seems out of sight.

Commitment has to be a resolve to fight through difficulties when others around you are criticizing you, when teammates are doubting you, or when your goal seems out of sight. Commitment is a strong belief in what you are doing and why you are doing it. It is what will get you past the challenges you encounter along the way. As we often tell our players: "We will always have a chance if our commitment is greater than the challenges, failures, and obstacles that are put before us."

BELIEF

We believe in players when they have
the grit to compete, can handle adversity
with great confidence, and handle success
with great humility.

JAY WRIGHT, NCAA CHAMPIONSHIP HEAD COACH,
VILLANOVA UNIVERSITY

We've all heard, "If you don't think you can … you're probably right." Or, "If you don't think you can … you won't."

If you don't first believe you have a chance of accomplishing something, there is no way you will actually accomplish it. Belief keeps the mind positive and the body resilient. Lack of belief keeps the mind in "doubt mode" and "hesitation mode." These are self-defeating.

But before we go much farther, you must understand that all achievers have a level of belief in themselves. It is equally as important to understand that belief is earned before it is acquired. Belief is not something you either have or don't have. It is something you have either earned or not earned. Belief requires lots of work.

This brings me to a word that many coaches and leaders do not seem to like: ego. We often hear that we want you to "leave your ego at the door." I could not disagree more. Ego is important; it's part of what got many of the best players to the level they have achieved.

Ego is needed … but it must be the winner's ego not the loser's ego!

The loser's ego is the kind that everyone complains about. It is the one we want people to leave at the door. In fact, I don't want those with loser's ego to leave it at the door, I don't even want them in the room. The loser's ego is focused on *me* and how good *I* am, not in the team or the team's success.

The winner's ego, by contrast, is a confidence in oneself—not cockiness—that is founded in all the work a person has put in before even arriving at the competition. It's knowing deep down that you have put enough sweat equity into yourself to allow you to know that you are prepared, and you are the best you can be. We want this kind of ego, as it provides the self-confidence needed to compete at the highest levels!

Teams who win have a belief in all parts of their programs. They believe in each other, in their coaches, and in the system they employ. Without belief, doubt creeps in. When doubt creeps in, hesitation seeps through. In an absence of belief in the system and in one another, teams become nothing more than a group of individuals. If you have too many with a *loser's ego*, the team will be hopelessly fractured.

So where does belief come from? It was best taught to me by the leadership team of the 212th Rescue Squadron when they explained why they believe in each other. They talked about how when you see every guy going through the rigorous training required of them, you start to understand that your teammates have invested in something more important than themselves. You watch every day how they do their part and work on improving the role they play in the larger success required of the group. You see proof that "I know this guy is ready; I know this guy will get it done; I have seen this guy fight through pressure, stress, mistakes, and still complete his mission; I believe in this guy and what he brings to our mission."

Going through tough times together, whether in training, practice, or live competition is very powerful; it provides evidence for what the group can accomplish together. This proof leads to the belief needed to be in the championship hunt.

Belief is not automatic. Saying you believe in yourself is insufficient. Belief comes about by providing reason to believe. For a team, that is measured in the work put in each day and in what we see in the guy next to us. For an individual, belief is found in the preparation, thought, and learning we do. Belief must always be preceded by consistent work. Only then can we be truly prepared for what we may face.

I saw the power of a leader's belief firsthand with Tyronn Lue and his ascension to the head-coaching position of the Cleveland Cavaliers. As Ty tells the story, "Doc Rivers was the first one to talk to me about becoming a head coach. He believed in me before I believed in myself. I really don't know what Doc saw in me."

What Doc saw was the knowledge Ty possessed, the sacrifices he made, and the work he put in as our defensive coordinator for the Los Angeles Clippers. What Doc also saw was a future head coach, but what he instilled was a belief in Ty that gave him the confidence to take the leap. The rest is history, as Ty's team went on to win the 2016 NBA championship in his first season!

UNREQUIRED

A lot of people notice when you succeed,
but they don't see what it takes to get there.

DAWN STALEY, 2017 NCAA CHAMPIONSHIP HEAD COACH,
UNIVERSITY OF SOUTH CAROLINA

I worry about this word a little bit. I know how important it is to success—but I worry about it because I think some people have a misguided conception of hard work. And some of that is because of what I call the "myths of success." These myths are things that we have been told since we were little kids, and that if we do them, then we will be successful.

As with many things in life, what was true in the past may not be so true today. Hard work does not guarantee success in today's competitive environment, because everyone is working hard. Hard work is the price of admission to get in the door that may or may not lead to your success.

John Calipari, the head coach of the University of Kentucky basketball team, was speaking to a group of young aspiring coaches at a clinic one summer in Las Vegas. I was there because the NBA Summer League is held there and our team was playing in it. I had heard that John was speaking at the conference and I knew I would walk away with some nuggets about success and growth. He did not disappoint, and one of his points was this: "There is a price to pay for every seat you want to occupy." If hard work is the price of admission, the price for the seat you want to occupy is even higher.

So, if possessing an earnest work ethic is expected, then what is the separator between being a hard worker and achieving success? The separator is doing the "unrequired work." The best of the best always do a little bit more. They work harder and more often. They do more than the people who they pass on the climb up the success ladder are willing to do. They deliver more than is expected and work more than contracts require. They do unrequired work.

> *The best of the best always do a little bit more. They work harder and more often. They do more than the people who they pass on the climb up the success ladder are willing to do.*

Kevin Garnett offers a great example. He may be one of the best defenders in the game, who never seems to get the recognition he deserves for the high level of individual and team defense he plays. One of the reasons he is so good is that he is so critical about his own defensive play. He self-assesses after every game and oftentimes during the course of the game.

I remember one practice when he must have felt that he needed more defensive repetitions. We were in what is called the Shell Drill. It is a four-on-four defensive drill where we break our defense down into its fundamental parts.

Doc usually liked to take Kevin out of a drill after five or six repetitions because he wanted to save Kevin's legs for games. Kevin had logged a lot of miles and wear and tear during his career, and he always practiced at game speed every minute we had him on the floor.

After five possessions Doc told one of our rookies, Leon Powe, to replace Kevin to give him a break. Kevin was not going to have any of that. As Leon said, "Kev, I got you," Kevin said he wasn't stopping, only in far-more colorful "KG" language. Leon turned to Doc and Doc told him again, "Take him out." Leon received another emphatic "NO" from Kevin. Finally, Doc had to nearly walk Kevin off the floor so we could get Leon in.

Once convinced to leave the drill, Kevin moved to the adjacent court, and as the eight players in the drill were talking and sliding and yelling out the defensive terminology each situation called for, we all heard another voice. The voice came from the other court, where Kevin was the only player. No other players, no ball, not a single other coach or person—just Kevin. There he was, sliding and talking and pretending to go through every action he would have had he still been in the actual drill. When the teams involved in the drill switched from defense to offense, so did Kevin. He yelled out all the offensive terms we employ: use me—use me; flash—flash—flash; rip—rip—rip.

What we learned that day watching and listening to Kevin was the true definition of unrequired work! Kevin knows that repetitions are what makes him one of the best at what he does. And like all successful people, he understands that his repetitions are what created his reputation. Or as I like to say "your reps create your rep!" Kevin's way of saying something similar was: "If you want to kick me out of a drill, you have to kick me out of the gym."

That day, Kevin gave an incredible success lesson to all of us that it's the unrequired work that will separate the great players and the great teams from all the rest. He didn't have to do that work. It wasn't work *required* of him. But he is Kevin Garnett because he does the unrequired work.

WOW! What if we all saw work ethic in this different light! How often would we reach our potential! How far could we go? How good would we feel about ourselves each night as we put our heads on our pillows?

CHOICES

Your choices are everything! Everything starts with a choice. There's a lot of "have to's" in life, but one thing that's in our power is our choices.

JAY BILAS, ESPN

What if we looked at our choices through different lenses? What if we looked at our choices not from the lens of what choices should we make, but rather through the one used by the most successful people, the lens of what will our choices make of us?

Every choice has a ripple effect that is the aftermath of that choice. The ripple can affect your team. The ripple can affect your teammates. The ripple can affect your status, your future, and your organization's future. The ripple effect is very real and must be given serious attention.

The second lens the best of the best look through is not just the effect it will have on them, but what effect will it have on their team and teammates? No one should make a choice that will reflect badly on himself or herself, but when in a team setting, the choice, if a player

> *The choice, if a player truly wants to win, must be made with the ripple effect in mind and what effect that choice will have on teammates and team.*

truly wants to win, must be made with the ripple effect in mind and what effect that choice will have on teammates and team. Thinking about the effects on those around you should be where your decisions start.

It is vitally important that you think about your choices and not just *make* your choices.

The ripple effect has been a part of my thinking for a long time. Every time I read an article about people who made a choice that came back to hurt them or their team I am reminded that I need to be more intentional about my choices.

This hit close to home when I was coaching with the Los Angeles Clippers. Blake Griffin, our all-star forward, made a choice that he still regrets. Blake, a teammate, and one of Blake's good friends who worked for the Clippers went out to eat in Toronto. Just as friends do, there was banter back and forth among the three of them. At one point the banter became personal and out of control and Blake reached across the table and punched his friend. It caused a serious injury to his friend's face and caused Blake to be fined by the team and suspended from games.

As many looked at this event, they most likely concentrated on the impact it had on Blake's bank account and the impact it had on the team when Blake was suspended. But the most damaging hit may have been to his reputation, because such actions do not reflect who Blake is. He is not normally someone who is going to hurt a friend like that. But that one time, he made the choice to reach over the table and throw the punch.

Here is the very important lesson for players, employees, coaches, and leaders. We all will be faced with choices every day— not usually the type of decision Blake faced, but choices nonetheless. As I often remind people, we are privileged to live in the United States, which allows us the freedom of choice. But the lesson is this: we may have the freedom of choice, but we do not have the freedom of the consequence.

> *We may have the freedom of choice, but we do not have the freedom of the consequence.*

Once Blake was one centimeter into his punch, he had no control of the consequences. Other people did. And the result was a major hit to his wallet and his reputation—not to mention our team.

No matter if you are an athlete, an employee, or in a leadership position, the choices you make often make you. Carefully consider each one. And always be certain that the choices you make are made through the lens of your values. This is the personal lens that guides us all. And this is a very, very powerful lens. Never make decisions that go against your value system. They almost never work, as we've seen with Bernie Madoff, Wells Fargo, or the recruiting scandal investigated by the FBI in college basketball. Each of these involved a breach of a value system. Whether it was greed that drove them or notoriety or trying to save a job, nothing should be more important than living by your values.

The more we give thought to what may seem like smaller decisions we face in our lives, the better prepared we will be to make thoughtful choices with consideration for lasting consequences when we encounter the big, difficult decisions.

CIRCLES

They must have a direct impact on your
growth by bringing a unique value. They must
bring out the best in you, challenge you,
energize you, and make you think.

**GEORGE RAVELING,
2015 BASKETBALL HALL OF FAME INDUCTEE**

A key question for all of us is: *Who are the people we are spending the most time with?*

This is something we may not give much conscious thought to, yet the people with whom we surround ourselves play a part in how we think, how we work, what attitude we bring to each day, and how we motivate ourselves. Those in our circle influence us in ways greater than we may think. Their influence can be positive or negative. George Raveling would often say that one of the biggest decisions we make each day is who we share our valuable time with.

Because that's true, it's important for us to be intentional about who we allow into our circle. And the question we all must ask ourselves when we evaluate who we are going to let in is not, "What can they do *for* me?" Their importance is not what they can do *for* you, but what they will do *to* you. This is the filter you must use to decide who gets in.

I have seen people whose circle has helped them in their careers, and in some cases, has been invaluable to their success. And I have, unfortunately, seen cases where a person's circle has really hurt him or her. More times than not, the circle has no understanding of the scope of responsibility we face or the difficult nature of decisions we must make every day. The people in it can't understand that a coach has a responsibility to the entire team and not just the individual player. They don't get that a CEO has to answer to the employees *and* the customers *and* the shareholders.

I have seen circles cause damage by

- making an individual believe he is better than he really is,
- making an individual turn on his or her teammates,
- enabling an individual to the point he or she feels entitled, and
- blaming the leader for an individual's poor performance.

In my basketball life I have seen circles of damage that include

- blaming the coach for not getting the player enough shots,
- blaming the coach for not getting the player more minutes, and
- blaming the organization for not getting the player enough publicity.

Your inner circle has to share a common objective and understand what it takes to succeed. You must form your inner circle from those who are in it for you and your gain—not for them and their gain. Circles have to be chosen wisely and must be filtered properly so that you are surrounded by those who know you and those who care for you. You need both to succeed.

As you create your circle, consider these filters:

- Choose people who will tell you the truth.
- Choose a circle that is small and tight knit; be very careful who you let in.
- Choose people who are wise, not just friendly.
- Choose people who will look out for your future, not just their future.
- Choose people who know what objectives you wish to reach and how to best reach them.
- Choose people who will help you not just take from you.
- Choose people who can inspire and impact your life and not just influence your life.
- Choose people "who know the no's" of success (no entitlement, no selfishness, no character mistakes).

Circles should not be based on friendship alone, but also on respect and trust. Do you respect the knowledge and experience of the people around you? Do you trust that they have your best interests at heart and not merely their own? Are they doing everything for you and making you lazy? Are they filling your mind with selfish thoughts and turning you against your teammates and/or your coach or leader? Are they convincing you that you can wait to do the work required of you tomorrow or the next day or the day after that?

Robert Kraft, the owner of the Super Bowl-Champion New England Patriots said, "The key to success in business and the key to life is creating aligned interests with smart people." If you add to that statement: "smart people who have your best interests at heart," then you have the key strategy to get you where you want to go.

Our circles touch us almost every day. They guide us through our most difficult times and decisions. These circles can be occupied by career enhancers or career killers.

Who do you need in your circle?

If you want to be great, put *serious* thought into who you will allow in your circles! You control the selection process.

COMPETITION

Elite competitors compete consistently and for longer periods of time than average competitors. They don't turn it on and off. They compete in everything they do, not just at game time.

KENNY ATKINSON, HEAD COACH, BROOKLYN NETS

Even though I often speak about building relationships and leading for others (and not for yourself), there is no denying there's competition in every industry, whether that is the heated rivalry between Apple and Microsoft, Ford and General Motors, or the two gas stations on opposite corners in your hometown. And many times, when you are really good at what you do, you will find that is when the competition is the fiercest. There will always be someone who wants to do what you do better than you do. Just as teams compete for earning the right to be declared champion, there is a company that wants to push your product out of the marketplace and a colleague who wants the same promotion you think you deserve. That's the nature of competition.

But competition is more than simply you against me. It is a mindset to bring the best that you have in you each day, no matter how things are going. Competitors get their reputations not from just playing or working hard; those are givens in the world of competition. True competition comes in when you are willing to continue to give the best of what you have even when you are losing. It's about giving all you have when the ordinary person would say, "This is too hard! Maybe I'll try again next game or with my next client or when I feel better." Competition doesn't wait for you to get better or feel better. Competitors compete when others give up. Competitors

> *True competition comes in when you are willing to continue to give the best of what you have even when you are losing.*

get past mad, sad, and hard. Becoming the best is supposed to be hard. Competition is supposed to test your best.

A competitor is one who doesn't change depending on the score. A competitor is one who gives honest, maximum effort at all times. A competitor gives the best of himself or herself until the finish. And regardless of what happened yesterday, a competitor gets up the next day and is ready to compete at his or her highest skill and energy level.

Competitors do not distinguish between venues. No matter if it's a practice or a game, they will compete. Whether they're starters or asked to be substitutes, they still compete. They may be assigned the high-visibility account or a low revenue account and they still bring their best in effort, mind, and skill. The venue, the level of the opponent, the amount of financial return does not matter. A competitor competes every time competition is part of the situation!

We were taught that lesson early in our championship season. Competitiveness struck us early, hard, and definitively in Rome, where the NBA had sent us to play two exhibition games. We decided to travel to Italy a few days early and conduct our training camp there.

In one of the first drills of our opening practice, our first unit (which included three all-stars and an emerging all-star) was going against our second unit in a full-court, scrimmage-like drill. Many would have observed that our second unit had no "name" players. But they did have a champion and that meant something to this group (and later our entire team understood its significance). James Posey had been on the NBA Champion Miami Heat in 2006. He knew what it took to win a title.

In this drill, the play got intense early on. At one point, the ball went out of bounds and the first unit felt it should be their ball. We all knew it actually went out off them, but they still argued. James had had enough and he went over to a first unit player, snatched the ball out of his arms, walked out of bounds, turned, and emphatically said, "OUR BALL. LET'S PLAY!"

To the outside world, this may not mean much, but for our team that year it said a lot. James let the first unit know that every day they are going to be challenged by the second unit, every day wasn't going to be just a practice. It was going to be a competition. James showed all of us that competition is the fuel that powers the engine of a championship-caliber team. He was not going to let anything slip ... not even a simple out-of-bounds call.

The competitor is driven to compete because that's what winners do—and it's what they owe their teammates, the fans, their coach, and the game itself. It should never be about the rewards, the adulation, or any financial returns.

PASSION

When love and purpose collide.

PJ FLECK, HEAD FOOTBALL COACH,
UNIVERSITY OF MINNESOTA

There's no question that passion is a key ingredient of success as an individual or a team. If you don't love what you're doing, there's no way you can get yourself through the difficult times. One lesson of sports is that its very nature is a journey of getting through difficult times. In high-level athletics, the physical strain, the emotional strain, the fact that there is always someone else who wants your spot, all pay a toll on the "is this worth it/can I do this anymore?" gauge. It's the passion that continues to put gas in your tank as the ups and downs of the season can cause you to run on empty at times.

John Welch is currently (2018) an assistant coach with the Los Angeles Clippers. He is known around the NBA world as one of the very best skill-development coaches in the game. He said something that speaks to passion: "It's hard to be good at something that you don't really like doing."

John's words remind us why we hear so many people talk about "finding our passion." But as I study successful people, I am convinced that passion often finds them. They aren't constantly looking for what it is they love. Keep your "passion antennas" up as you go through life, and be ready to seize whatever it is that keeps you excited. When that passion finds you, you will discover that it becomes the last thing you think about before you go to sleep and the first thing you think about when you wake up.

I did not go out and search for basketball. As a young boy, basketball was just something guys were playing. It simply appeared in one of my days, and after playing the game with my friends I left the court that day thinking no more than, "This is fun. I liked doing it." I wasn't good at it, I did not understand it, but I had fun doing it. Because I enjoyed basketball, I put in the work to become good at it and, eventually, to understand it at the levels required to be a coach. Passion doesn't come into your life as passion. Passion's introduction is the "like-it" stage. Then like it grows to "really enjoy it." Which grows to "love it." Which finally becomes passion. And that's where we get the line we often hear from very successful people when they say: "I feel like I haven't worked a day in my life." That, to me, is passion.

Passion can be the difference in a young player making it or not making it, as coaches love players who love the game, the sweat, and the gym. But you can't ride passion forever if you want to succeed. At some point your knowledge has to catch up with your passion. The best players are the ones who understand this. They are the ones who continue to learn, continue to find ways to grow, continue to listen when something is being taught, continue to take the teaching and see it not as criticism but as the coaching they need to be successful. When your knowledge catches up with your passion, that's when the magic really happens.

Successful teams understand that passion is not just important to the individual, it is also important to the team. Lesson twelve of the eighteen lessons of Colin Powell's "Leadership Primer" states: "Perpetual optimism is a force multiplier."

I believe if you substitute passion for the word optimism, you can see the effect passion has not only on an individual, but on a team. Passion brings a spirit to a team, and all winning teams will tell you that the spirit of their team is important. Kevin Garnett's passionate play often got us over the hump in games when the outcome could have gone either way. His passion was the difference maker on those nights because his passion was contagious.

I have heard people say that you can see passion, but I know from coaching Kevin for six years, you can *feel* passion. It was this contagious feeling that brought everyone into Kevin's passion and gave us the energy we didn't know we had in us on a given night. Where some players may be too cool to be passionate, the best of the best don't care about cool. To them, passion is critical.

Many believe passion often comes from those on the bench, thinking that since they don't play much they must really love the game. Passion cannot just reside on your bench, it has to be seen and felt on the floor. If it's present and shared through your best players, it becomes that force multiplier Colin Powell was talking about. When you have a team of passionate players and combine it with mastering skills and accepting roles, you have a team that has a legitimate shot at championship-level play!

Doc Rivers has a great saying about succeeding at the highest level and going after something that deep down you really want. All playoff teams covet something that only one team, the best team, can win: the Larry O'Brien Trophy. During the playoffs, Doc often reminded us, "Sometimes you have to put your heart into something knowing full well that it could be broken." The best part about passion and why it is so important to success is that passion allows us to put ourselves out there even when we know that failure may be the result.

Passion is all about putting your entire heart into something. The best of the best continue to give the whole of their hearts after

> *The best part about passion and why it is so important to success is that passion allows us to put ourselves out there even when we know that failure may be the result.*

losses, after disappointments, even after embarrassments, and yes, even in practices! They reach deep inside, put their heart back into their effort, and get after it one more time!

All great individuals and all great teams have a passion for what they are doing. They bring a positive spirit to the day. And positive spirit is also a force multiplier. It has a way of bringing others into the positive mindset and away from the negativity that often resides in losing individuals and losing teams. As bestselling author, Jon Gordon, says in his great book *The Energy Bus,* "Don't be an energy vampire!" Vampires suck the positive out of offices and locker rooms. On the other extreme from the energy vampire is the passion provider. Bring your passion every day and see where it takes your team or your company. Be that Passion Provider for your team.

Passion is a valuable part of successful people's make-up—because success is hard. Success demands tests like failure and embarrassment. The drive to get through both of these is passion. Passion allows us to keep coming back. In tough times "just a job" is hard to do every day of the year, but a "passion for the job" gives us the positive momentum to push through the difficult times. Passion is the ingredient that allows our love for something to be greater than the periods of grind we go through, the challenges we face, and the failures we experience. Passion provides the resilience needed to "get past" and "get through." Just like discipline, passion gets you through those days that are the hardest. And passion fights off the lingering effects of those days. Passion has a cleansing effect. It's passion that gets you back on the positive track.

A note of caution, however: passion is not just the "rah-rah" voice or the emotional outbursts. Rah-rah is often short lived, and becoming emotional is not what we want. The key is to perform with emotion, not get emotional.

Use passion, but more importantly, let the passion simply exude from you. That is when it is most powerful. That is when it will offer the greatest contribution to winning!

HABITS

There's no big secret to success in
the NBA. The secret is there is no secret.
It's just boring old habits.

**RAY ALLEN, 2018 HALL OF FAME,
NBA CHAMPION BOSTON CELTICS**

How important are habits? Many will say they are what we fall back on. While I agree in part, I also believe they are much more important than that. I believe they are what we rely on in our most difficult moments of stress, pressure, and uncertainty.

We must first acknowledge that there are two types of habits we can choose to make a part of our lives—good ones and bad ones. The good ones are often harder to choose and put into practice, but they are also more rewarding. They're the intentional habits that help get us to where we want to go with our lives and careers.

I say the word "choose" intentionally, as the habits we form are a direct result of the choices we make. We have the ultimate say in the habits we form. And it has been proven time and time again that the best of the best have developed good habits and are always working to eliminate bad ones.

The key for us is to find out what those good habits are and to do our best to replicate them within ourselves. We must make sure they are a part of us so that they become who we are and not just what we do. These could be nutritional habits. They could be mindset habits. They could be workout habits. They could be reading habits.

Championship-caliber athletes understand that it is their mind, their skill, and their body that will determine their success. Most young athletes only think of the skill set. To be the best requires going beyond skills. As you climb the ladder, you find that everyone has mastered skills or they would not be where they are. Now you have to find ways to separate yourself from others. That separation often comes with your body (nutrition and working out) and your mind (having the right mindset to become the best).

Habits come down to a decision followed by a daily repetition of what's needed. Habits take time. In order to grow, I made the decision to learn more about leadership. I started reading and researching on a daily basis. I then put some new thing I learned into my leadership style as often as I could.

It is not easy to create a new habit, as the best ones are demanding. But as we go through the "hard" we must keep in front of our minds the reminder that most others, including our competitors, are not likely to commit to forming a new habit. They will not be willing to get past hard or inconvenient or pass up something that may be more fun. They may try every now and then, but they will not commit. This commitment to habit is your separator!

One of the greatest to ever play basketball was Kobe Bryant. Kobe has talked about one of the habit separators for him—coming in at 4:00 a.m. He committed to being there at that early hour to get his first workout in before anyone else. This was his mindset habit. The work he put in on the simple parts of the game are legendary. He would work on the fundamentals: perfect the form on his jump shot, the exact footwork on his jab step. These were the skill-set habits he was making sure were part of his game. While others become

> *While others become bored with the basics, Kobe made a habit of mastering them, working every day to turn those basics into separators.*

bored with the basics, Kobe made a habit of mastering them, working every day to turn those basics into separators.

One of the things I did for Nike Basketball was to direct the Nike Skills Academy for the best high school and college players in the country. We would teach them and drill them on the fundamentals and concepts of the game over three days. We broke them down by position, and each position had an NBA player as the guest pro. Our first year we had Kobe Bryant fulfill that role as a great wing player.

Kobe's camp was held in Los Angeles, and we had another coach running that site. I was in Boston running the site where Paul Pierce was the guest pro.

Alan Stein, one of the coaches we hired at the LA site, tells the story of wanting to observe one of Kobe's individual workouts for himself so that he could not only see Kobe's work but also feel its intensity. And believe me he saw and felt both. But it was a little different than he thought it might be. For two hours he witnessed Kobe working on the most basic of drills, drills you might see your junior high child doing. And he did them over and over and over again. He worked on a fundamental until he felt he got it right. Kobe knew the fundamentals would be the habits he would fall back on during the most important and challenging parts of a game.

At the end of the workout Alan had to find out why Kobe focused so heavily on basic drills, so he posed this question: "Kobe, you are the *best* player in the world. Why would you spend two hours on some of the most fundamental drills in the game and do them over and over again?" Kobe's answer: "Why do you think I am the best player in the world?"

What a lesson on habits and the importance of turning the fundamentals of the game into a habit of success. The drills Kobe practiced formed the foundation that allowed him to do all of the extraordinary things he did in a game.

Kobe understood the secret to greatness. The secret is that there is no secret. It is the habit of working on the fundamentals of your craft so that, when necessary, you can go beyond the fundamentals and make the incredible play that leaves people saying, "That was just luck." Only it won't be luck at all! It's about what allows luck to happen: habits, work, and preparation!

URGENCY

Every day I make sure we give a damn!

MIKE RHOADES, HEAD COACH,
VIRGINIA COMMONWEALTH UNIVERSITY

T he best of the best understand the importance of *the now*—this possession, this repetition, this drill, this report, this action, this phone call. Everything that must be done on this day at this time at this moment is what urgency is all about. While average players and average people feel that "this" play doesn't matter in the greater scheme of things, the best performers understand that a presence of urgency is how they gain separation from their competition. They take care of the now.

We live in a time when everything is changing at a far more rapid pace than ever before. To keep up with such a pace demands urgency in individuals, teams, and organizations. We must make decisions between complacency to stay status quo or urgency to stay ahead. Yet we must understand that urgency does not mean going as fast as we can and being reckless. Winning urgency is an attitude of now. Being prepared now. Getting things done now. Coming up with the next best thing now. As we often said at Nike Basketball: get to the future first. Urgency is a must if winning is the goal.

I had the opportunity to speak to GE Healthcare employees in Logan, Utah and spend time with their CFO for upstream bioprocessing, Jeff Jackman. He opened my eyes on the subject of

88 · **WHY** THE BEST ARE THE **BEST**

urgency. He said, "When I think of urgency I think of speed. People can get burned out with too much urgency. The best urgency comes not from management forcing it on people, not from a dictatorial approach, but from creating a culture where passion thrives and translates into people wanting to get the work done when it needs to be done."

Jeff sees urgency as a joint decision to create a timeline that works for the company and the employee. "As a leader I see urgency as my way of helping them prioritize, and sometimes you will have to challenge the deadline they want. You just have to be careful how you deliver an urgency request." And, knowing Jeff, he delivers it in a respectful way. The best leaders understand respect often eliminates the resentment that might be felt from a forced timeline.

In the book *Good to Great,* Jim Collins writes about a basic principle that good is the enemy of great. Just as that is true, so too is procrastination the enemy of growth, development, improvement, and accomplishment.

It took me a long time to understand that urgency is a habit. It is something that we all can make a part of our lives. If we are intentional about doing things now, paying attention to what is happening now, executing fundamentals the way they should be executed now, and putting the energy into the game or the project now, we will all be farther along our journey to success.

Maybe the best way to think about urgency is this: the more you put thoughts like "tomorrow and later" before actions like

> *Maybe the best way to think about urgency is this: the more you put thoughts like "tomorrow and later" before actions like "right now, immediately, at this moment," the more you will fall behind your competitors.*

"right now, immediately, at this moment," the more you will fall behind your competitors *and* in fulfilling the dreams that you have for your life, your company, or your team.

Jon Gordon's book *One Word* is all about choosing one word as your word for the year. That word becomes a trigger that will get your mind to the place you need it to be. For example, I chose the word *now* as one of my success words for 2018. Throughout that year, I kept this word in front of mind every day. The word served as my "catch-me" reminder when I got the urge to put something off. As soon I thought of the word *now*, I shifted into "urgency mode."

All of us have said, "I will get to it tomorrow. I will get to it on Monday. I will get to after this TV show. I will get to it on January 1." If you live in the world of "get to it," you most likely will also be living in the world of "never will" or "too late."

I have taken the meaning behind this word to an extreme: as I am watching a game or a TV show, at each commercial break I will get something done. I might do ten push-ups. I could do twenty sit-ups. I might move the wash to the dryer. Or take a plate to the sink. But I take action that will keep me in the *now*. Whatever it is, it will be something that solidifies urgency as a staple of my daily life.

STANDARDS

*We set our standards very high and we don't
apologize for that. We embrace that.*

**MUFFETT MCGRAW, NCAA NATIONAL
CHAMPIONSHIP HEAD COACH, NOTRE DAME**

February 2010. Los Angeles, California. Staples Center Arena. The Lakers had beaten us on our home court earlier in the year. We only play the Lakers twice a year, home and away. We had been playing pretty well but we knew we had more in us. We looked at the marathon of an NBA season as a gradual building process. We wanted to build the confidence of our team and the execution of our system continuously and consistently throughout the year. People's perceptions were that we could not let them sweep us in the regular season and gain that mental edge. We needed what many thought was a signature win. This time around, I was in agreement with popular perception.

The forty-eight minutes following tip-off may have been one of the most intense games I have ever coached. There were elbows to the face, jabs to the gut, shoulders to the chest. There was smack talking. There was a display of every competitive edge one could employ.

When the final buzzer sounded, I looked up at the scoreboard: Los Angeles 86 … Boston 87!

I was thinking, "We got our signature win!" I had to play it cool on the outside, as this was "just" the regular season. But inside

I was pumped up. I could not wait for Doc to deliver the postgame message: We are set. We are ready. We just beat the Lakers! I knew we were in for a special message, something Doc was phenomenal at every time he spoke.

As soon as the game was over, we walked back through the wood-paneled hallways of the Staples Center until we reached our locker room door. Like any other game, the coaches got there before most of the players. This is when, as a coaching staff, we complete a quick game review and Doc gives us a sense of what his message will be. It can be a true learning/teaching message or it can be a simple "Let's get out of here and get on the plane as quickly as we can." But this time was different. I could see him still formulating his thoughts. As we were standing there as a staff, our backs were to the locker room door, but we heard the excitement of each player as he entered. We felt the wind gusts of some of the players who were actually sprinting down the hallway and into the locker room.

Doc said, "Let's go." I reached out to turn the doorknob of the locker room door when I felt a hand grasp my wrist. It was Doc. He said: "I don't like the vibe. We're too giddy. We still have four more months of this." I can remember thinking that four months led us out to June. Then it hit me. He was already thinking NBA finals.

> *I can remember thinking that four months led us out to June. Then it hit me. He was already thinking NBA finals.*

We entered the locker room, and Doc said: "Great game tonight, guys. We got what we came here to get, a win on their court. But guys, this is only February. We still have two more months of the regular season to go and the playoffs after that."

He continued with a brilliant motivational and leadership tactic.

He said, "I want everyone in this room to give me $100 right now. Give it to Kevin. Here's what we are going to do. We are going to hide it in this locker room and we are going to come back in June and get our money back." Those were his words, but what he really signaled was that we were going to be in the NBA finals again—and we were not only going to come back to get our money, we were going to come back and get the ring.

History will show the Lakers won the ring that year. But the tactic worked, as it set a new standard for our team that night. We were not going to be satisfied with a standard of just winning regular-season games. Not only would our standards be much higher, we would play up to and against our standards, not just play the opponent!

> *The tactic worked, as it set a new standard for our team that night.... Not only would our standards be much higher, we would play up to and against our standards, not just play the opponent!*

What are you willing to accept from yourself with the work you put in each day? From the way you act every day? From the way you lead? It's the answers to these questions that will set you up for either success or failure. Your standards define not only what you will strive to reach but also the levels you will not tolerate from yourself.

I believe there are three forms of competition that challenge us to be our best:

1. Competing against an opponent.

2. Competing against the clock.

3. Competing against ourselves.

The best do all three but emphasize the third. Competing against ourselves is actually competing against our own personal standards. If your standards are high enough, wins and losses usually take care of themselves.

High standards are synonymous with successful teams and athletes. They are the guiding push we need when the pull to do less challenges us. And that pull enters all of our lives at some point. The key is to *live up* to those standards and never *play down* to the standards and levels of the opponents we face or the people we may be working with. As Jay Bilas once said to me, "The key is to not just to get *through* your day, it's to get *from* your day."

It's when you are playing those teams you know you should beat that standards are most needed. Standards challenge you to play up to the level of your talent; up to the level of your role; up to the level of a champion. Not down to the level of your opponent. Winning the battle against the high standards you set may be even more important. Time and time again I have seen teams focus on playing to the standards they have established and found that the score truly does take care of itself.

What might these standards look like? Here they are—the standards the Celtics players set for themselves and lived by each day.

Boston Celtics:
Standards Of Excellence

1. **PROFESSIONALISM:** we will commit to always conducting ourselves in a first-class manner on and off the court every day of the year; this is a twenty-four-hour, seven-days-a-week commitment; we understand there is a difference between being in the pros and being a professional!

2. **NO PERSONAL AGENDAS:** we will commit to one agenda and one agenda only; that agenda will be doing whatever we are called on to do in order to help this team win a championship; our personal gains or situations will never come into play!

3. **PROFESSIONAL AND RESPECTFUL COMMUNICATION:** we will commit to listening to the "what" and not the "how"; but will always be aware of how we are sending the message; let it be teammate to teammate and delivered with respect!

4. **THINK OF THE NOW ONLY:** we will commit to making sure everything we do is for the betterment of THIS TEAM THIS YEAR; our personal situations will take a back seat to the team commitment!

5. **ONE WAY:** we will commit to the teaching and the system that we have, trusting the coaching and holding yourself accountable to do things the CELTIC WAY!

6. **EFFICIENT TEAM:** we will commit to executing our system with simplicity to ensure that we are productive and efficient in everything we do!

7. **TEAM OF EXECUTION:** we will commit to learning our system; understanding our system, and paying attention to the details of our system, understanding that when two equal teams meet—the team that executes better usually wins!

8. **NEVER HAVE A BAD PRACTICE:** we will commit to giving our best effort every day we hit the practice floor, at times understanding that we will have to pick our teammates up when needed! We can never get bored with the process!

9. **RESPONSIBILITY:** we commit to holding ourselves personally responsible and accountable for our actions, our efforts, and in fulfilling the roles that we have been assigned; everyone will take responsibility for their role in our success!

10. **TRUST:** we will commit to this on a twenty-four-hour basis, trusting each other in everything we do on and off the court, from talking on defense to trusting that guys are getting their rest and taking care of their bodies to trusting that everyone is representing each other in a first-class manner at all times!

11. **NO EXCUSES:** we either get it done or we don't; either way, we move on and make sure the next possession, the next quarter, the next game is up to CELTIC STANDARD!

12. **GET IT RIGHT:** we must understand it's more important to get it right than for you to be right!

COURAGE

efore I get into courage and how I believe it applies to success, I want to make a few distinctions on the levels of courage relative to different situations. I have always associated courage with people who put themselves in harm's way. When I think of courage I think of our military and police and their courageous commitment to protect us and do so in dangerous situations. I think of the courage of the single parent working multiple jobs, fighting each day to provide for his or her children. And what about that December day in 1955 when Rosa Parks walked onto that bus in Montgomery, Alabama? Imagine the courage *that* took!

I am hesitant to include courage in the context of coaching, leadership, and success in the face of such comparisons. But looking at it through the lens of each, I do believe there is application. It may not be at the same level as the examples above, but courage is required to take certain next steps in our lives and careers.

There are different levels of courage that many successful people have displayed. I have often categorized these levels as:

- **"Loss-of-Life" courage**: the men and women of our military.

- **"Fight-For" courage**: Rosa Parks fighting for social justice.

- **"Reputational" courage**: making a decision that, if wrong, could cost us public embarrassment or even the loss of our livelihood.

- **"Fear-Of" courage**: taking on that new job, giving that first presentation in front of the toughest client you have.

I love the story of Beth Mowins, the first female play-by-play announcer to call a nationally televised NFL game. Beth's goal since childhood was to call games on TV. I had a conversation with her about the courage to climb the success ladder in the male-dominated profession of sports announcing. Beth told me that courage for her was "the ability to have a dream and chase that dream." She said, "I had no fallback plan, as I really had nothing else I wanted to do career-wise. So my courage was to step into the fray and put myself out there."

That passion helped her overcome and gave her the courage, but preparation also played a huge part. If she had any fear at all it was "when that moment came I wouldn't be at my best. So, I over-prepare to the point that when I walk into that booth for NFL football I *know* I am ready." Preparation, readiness, and courage trumps fear.

> *Sometimes courage manifests itself in trusting your instincts even when you know you will face ridicule if those instincts prove wrong.*

Sometimes courage manifests itself in trusting your instincts even when you know you will face ridicule if those instincts prove wrong. We witnessed Nick Saban's reputational courage in the January 2018 college football championship game. At halftime, he felt they needed a boost of some kind. His decision was to change quarterbacks and insert backup Tua Tagovailoa to start the second half. Why was this a gamble? The guy he came in for, Jalen Hurts, guided them through the year and into this championship game through his stellar play. It was a decision that had risk written all over it. If this decision failed, Coach Saban would have had to face some pretty severe public ridicule to say the least. Everyone would have been questioning his judgment, and critics might wonder, "Has the game passed him by?"

To take such a risk is a characteristic of reputational courage, something the best of the best do with regularity. Like many decisions of this type, it presented a high level of risk and an equally high level of reward. Coach Saban and the Alabama football team got the reward that night! What we all saw was why Nick Saban is always in the discussion as the best college football coach in history.

The best of the best are driven by the courage of their convictions. They are not scared off by popular opinion. They are driven by educated decisions. Clearly, Coach Saban had already thought about this possibility as evidenced by his postgame remarks. It was more than a gut decision, even if it may have come from the gut.

Courage has nothing to do with how tough you are physically and everything to do with how strong you are mentally. Everyone wants to be the person in charge or the best player, but not everyone understands those positions often require decisions that could lead people to question your ability to even hold such a position.

In the talks I give on leadership, I break down the "Will Be's" of leadership. Leadership does not guarantee 100 percent agreement just because you said it, and it needs the courage to stand by your convictions. Understand that as a leader:

- You *will be* critiqued from inside and outside the organization!

- You *will be* questioned from inside and outside the organization!

- You *will be* criticized from inside and outside the organization!

Based on these "Will Be's," you must have the courage to stick with what you believe to be right. Courage becomes important in success in that you have to believe when no one else believes and you have to have the strength to act on these beliefs and stay with them in the face of public or internal scrutiny. But if you have put in study, research, and thought to the decision, you have the right to believe in it and the courage to execute it.

In my consulting work for a professional sports team, I was joined by another consultant who was a special advisor to President Barack Obama. At the end of one of the sessions, I asked him to describe President Obama in one sentence. His reply: "He has the intellectual curiosity to get to the best solution and the courage to stand by it."

President Obama knew that he alone controlled all the necessary thought and discussion behind the decision. That controlling factor was his curiosity to find the best solution. He then earned the right to believe in that solution. But he knew this is where courage must show its face—to get over the hump of questioning yourself and over the hump of that fear of potential failure. Courage doesn't mean you are free from fear. It means you take action anyway. You get past scared. This is where courage gets its definition (or at least *my* definition of it): When the necessary work you put in meets the conviction of purpose you have, courage is formed!

CURIOSITY

Keeps people dreaming and that
can be a great thing!

**PAUL GARTLAN,
PRESIDENT AND CEO, SKYBOX CHECKOUT**

For the last twenty-five years, I have been talking to coaches all over the world about a very important decision they have to make if they want to give themselves a chance to succeed. I tell them that there are two types of people in this world:

1. Know–it–alls

2. Learn–it–alls

We all have to decide which type we are going to be. And that holds true for individuals as well as companies and sports teams. There is no doubt that the only way to grow, develop, and improve is to be a learn–it–all, to have a curiosity about what else is still left to learn, left to do, and left to develop.

The world is moving so fast. Customers demand more and demand it now. The pace of work and production has become the new way of life. Next, new, better, and faster are the common demands we face. We must continue to learn if we want to keep up. I call the desire to do so the "curiosity gene."

I have coached many of the best players in the game, and they all have this curiosity gene. They want to know everything they can about what will make them better, what will help make them grow, what will allow them to become a better version of their current self. Phil Jackson once told Kobe Bryant that he needed to study the best of the best in different professions to find out what they did to become the best. Learn what made them who they are, he told Kobe. Kobe, being who he is, took that to heart and cold-called people at the pinnacle of their professions to ask them what they did to become so good at what they do.

I saw the same desire in LeBron James that day at Nike when I apologized for pushing him hard. He responded, "I'm good. I want to know everything I need to know to get better." That day with LeBron, I learned the formula for how the great ones think. They know they can't reach success on their own or with their current knowledge. They have to keep learning in order to keep growing. Remember this formula we discussed when talking about truth? *Better + Better + Better + Better = Becoming Your Best.*

> *Curiosity is the foundation for getting better—the curiosity to learn how you can improve, try new ways of doing things, and learn how to remain relevant. But it doesn't happen overnight; improvement is a drip–drip–drip, get better–get better–get better proposition.*

Curiosity is the foundation for getting better—the curiosity to learn how you can improve, try new ways of doing things, and learn how to remain relevant. But it doesn't happen overnight; improvement is a drip–drip–drip, get better–get better–get better proposition.

When I think of people with a curious mind, I often think of Carl Liebert, the executive vice president and COO of USAA, the mission-based company that serves our military by providing a full range of financial services to keep their members financially secure. Carl is a consummate lifelong learner and will tell you this has been key to his success in leadership positions.

He believes this mindset is connected to his servant/leadership philosophy, and he takes this role very seriously. It is not just a position—it's a responsibility. In his words, one of his responsibilities as a senior executive is "to learn something new each year that can impact the organization." To learn something that he can then share with his teammates to create a bigger impact on the military community they serve. The more he learns the more he can give back.

One way he goes about this is to "remain intellectually curious." He believes if you are not intellectually curious, then you're not constantly learning—and in fact you are falling behind. Carl keeps a constant feed of books, podcasts, blogs, news articles, and Ted Talks in rotation to quench his insatiable thirst for knowledge.

He has created what he calls "Summer School" where he sets three to four days aside each summer to learn something new or to delve into a subject he feels needs a deeper dive. Recent Summer School trips have taken him on learning journeys to Amazon, Google, Tesla, Microsoft, and many start-ups to find out more about the agility of IT structures, artificial intelligence, and big data. One Summer School session took him to the Stanford Design School to study human-centered design. The goal always remains to bring knowledge back to share with the team, so that everyone learns. As a former naval officer, he ties his philosophy to a nautical saying, "a rising tide lifts all boats."

He also uses a week of his summer vacation to work Mike Krzyzewski's summer basketball camp at Duke. Sure, it's a great time to be with his kids as they participate, and Carl gives back as a coach in the camp, but he also gets to sit at the same table each day and ask questions of one of the greatest coaches of all time. He loves it and "takes feverish notes as Coach K talks about leadership and team building."

Carl holds a senior-leadership position, but leaders don't have a monopoly on curiosity and learning. Any of us can exercise our curiosity gene. Every professional player I have ever worked with has had and used this gene. Coach K even has his own Sirius XM Radio show where he interviews successful people and takes his own notes as he shares their views with listeners.

People like Coach K and Carl don't follow the long-held belief: "If you can't beat them, join them." That is not the thought process of the best; they believe: if you can't beat them, learn from them!

I once texted Erik Spoelstra, currently (2018) the head coach of the Miami Heat, asking him how he would best describe what made the legendary Pat Riley (Hall of Fame coach and current [2018] president of the Heat) successful? How would Erik describe Pat? I purposely texted Erik because I wanted a concise, pointed description of who Pat Riley is. Erik had worked with Pat Riley for more than twenty years, so I thought if anyone would have the best answer, he would.

Here is what Erik texted back: *"In his office; at his desk; dimly lit; his coffee, his blue hard stock paper, his pen; and alone with his thoughts."*

Now that might not be the answer you would expect, but I found this description to be every bit as powerful as it was visual. I saw something about what makes the best the best. The takeaway was not that Pat likes coffee, nor that he doesn't like bright lights, nor that he has to have hard stock blue paper. What I took away was that Pat was "alone with his thoughts."

This world we live in is so fast-paced and high-pressured that we always put ourselves in action mode. We are on that proverbial treadmill and do not know how to get off nor how to stop it. It's day after day after day nonstop. But what I have found is that the best of the best make sure they find time to simply think. They find time to pursue curiosity, sort out options, massage an idea to make it the best for the given situation, to put sustained thought to difficult decisions in order to bring greater clarity to the final decision. They get off the treadmill and find a private spot to do what needs to be done: think!

> *The best of the best make sure they find time to simply think. They find time to pursue curiosity, sort out options, massage an idea to make it the best for the given situation.*

Porter Moser, the head coach at Loyola University Chicago, told me that thinking allows him to slow down, to soak things in better, to be more thoughtful, to better enjoy a moment and make more of an impact on the moment. I call what Moser talks about "Think Time," and I incorporate it into every day. I have to make time to just think. Intentional thinking is a discipline. You have to make time for it, and you have to make a commitment to it.

Once Think Time becomes a habit, you will never want to go a day without it. Such focus allows you to dig deeper into your mind and spend the uninterrupted time not only to find ways to avoid the mistakes of the past, but to clear your head and execute in the present—and to develop a curious, imaginative mind that allows you to envision the future.

In any difficult job there will be tough decisions. There will always be circumstances in which you must anticipate the best course of action required for the future. These decisions are best made when the emotion and the pressure of the moment are not present in your thoughts. That is the pre-thought Jerry West spoke about back in the

"Truth" section of this chapter. That is Think Time. Thinking allows us to disregard opinion and contemplate information. It allows us to move beyond emotions and reach logic.

George Raveling always talks about Phil Knight, Nike's founder, as a thinker and one who reflects. He said that Phil Knight taught him to

- think what others won't think;
- go where others won't go;
- do what others won't do; and
- be what others want to be.

Thinking is the foundation of Knight's advice! For me, I make sure to find thirty to sixty minutes a day to just think!

The best of the best realize they don't know all they need to know and don't have all the answers they hope to have. How do they solve this challenge? Intellectual Curiosity! They build "think time" into their lives and remain hungry for new knowledge.

RESPECT

Having respect in this league is one of the hardest
things to do. It's not just about how you perform but
how hard you work. Hard work gives you respect.

KEVIN GARNETT, 2008 NBA CHAMPION, BOSTON CELTICS

I n my thirteen years coaching in the NBA with and against
some of the greatest to play the game, I noticed that the great
ones all received respect—and they also gave it back to their
teammates, their coaches, their opponents, and the game.

They received respect because they earned it first. Respect is
always earned before it is given. Respect has nothing to do with what
you think of your game. Respect is about what you have proven
through the work and sacrifice you put in and the results you have
achieved. When others notice your and your teammates' effort and
dedication, only then do they grant you their respect. Receiving the
respect of your competitors and teammates, no matter your profession, should be your ultimate goal.

In my time in the NBA, I noticed
something else. The great players who
received respect also gave respect. They
were on their best game each night
because they respected the fact that
their opponent would be on their best
game as well. They respected that their

> *In my time in the
> NBA, I noticed
> something else. The
> great players who
> received respect
> also gave respect.*

opponents earned their way to the professional level and that on any given night they had enough talent to beat them.

The professionals of the NBA respected their teammates because they knew they could not achieve personal success without benefiting from team success. They respected the work and time that their teammates put into the game no matter their role or level of talent. Thinking about the work and effort teammates bring each day, remembering that they will bring their best effort each night, reminds the player that he must bring his best. The best players respect this dual responsibility.

They respected the coaches for their time, effort, and dedication. They respected the demands of success. And finally, they respected the game. They came to understand that the game was played by talented, hard-working players and coached by talented, hard-working coaches, and no matter your own talent and preparation, you could be beaten on any given night. Respect for the game allowed them to stay on top of their own game because they knew everything could change at any minute. One injury, one trade, one coaching change, and the game could be taken away. They respected the fact that the game can humble you.

They also understood that the game gave them a lot in return.

Ultimately, we have to look at respect as more than a word and think in terms of what respect does for us. Respect:

- creates awareness;
- provides a warning; and
- gives us inner strength.

As a coach observing players' relationships with their teammates, opponents, and with the game itself, I also discovered that respect diminishes the possibility of being upset by an inferior opponent. Respect helps you reach your potential. Respect ensures that you bring your best every night.

ADJUSTMENT

To remain successful, you have to continually
adjust and evolve. If you only bring the same thing
all the time, the competition will catch up and end
up beating you. You have to find that fine balance
between making those timely adjustments and
staying committed to your time-tested beliefs.

**ERIK SPOELSTRA, NBA CHAMPIONSHIP COACH,
MIAMI HEAT**

We live in an ever-changing world, and the old saying that you've got to change with it holds true. For example, in the NBA at the turn of this century, you didn't need a guy who could guard three positions; today you can't compete without those kinds of defenders. Although I think change, sometimes even wide-scale change, is critical to sustainability in sports and business, I want to speak to the idea of *adjustment* instead ...

But first, one more thing on change: to sustain we must change. We may not like it, but we have to live with it, and even more than live with it, we have to make it work. I often share this saying: "We have to make it work while we're seeing if it works."

This goes for Apple and the changes Steve Jobs made when he came back to the company or a sports team when they trade a player who may have been important and well respected. Both cases require the teams to make it work. Just as with any change, success is not guaranteed. Change is a researched, educated guess/hope for the future sustainability of the organization. In order to give it a chance to work everyone has to try to make it work.

But enough on change; let's get to this word *adjustment*.

> *Adjustments are those subtle tweaks we have to make when the game plan may not be working as well as we thought it would. These may include a substitution, a schematic change, or even an addition to an offensive or defensive emphasis.*

Adjustments are those subtle tweaks we have to make when the game plan may not be working as well as we thought it would. These may include a substitution, a schematic change, or even an addition to an offensive or defensive emphasis.

One of my mentors, Hal Nunnally, a longtime coach from Randolph-Macon College, once said to me, "The four most important words in coaching are, 'Shit, it ain't working.'" His lesson is that if you want to lead, you must be able to see and adjust.

Basketball is not a game of perfect, nor is coaching or leadership. We have to be able to adjust. But I caution you here—we should not adjust after every time something doesn't work because if we believe in *everything*, we believe in *nothing*.

Tom Thibodeau was our defensive coordinator the year we won the title in Boston. I will never forget his best advice on adjustments. He said, "Before we adjust anything, we have to first make sure we are doing it the way we have taught it." His strategy for adjustment was to let the players know that we will have some checks before we adjust: "First we needed to do it harder, then do it better" We were going to make darn sure it was done the correct way before we were going to make an adjustment. How do we know if something truly isn't working if we aren't doing it right and doing it at game speed?

The takeaway is this: We spent many hours and many years coming up with a system we knew would work and give our team the best chance to be successful. Because of the research, study, thought, and time to come up with this system, we developed a strong belief in it. Why would we change it just because it didn't work a few times? We first have to see if we are doing it our way before we change.

As it often turned out, the most needed change was more in the areas of effort and execution. Which takes me to my last point about Thib's philosophy. If you don't try to do it harder and you don't do it any better, then we should take you out!

Adjustment is all about the "what-if" preparation you put in prior to having to execute your plan. What if they do this? What if this doesn't work? What if this player gets in foul trouble? That same wise mentor, Coach Nunnally, also used to say, "The coach who wins is the coach who is prepared for and is willing to make that second adjustment."

I start out with a plan. My opponent takes action to counter that plan. I then adjust to his adjustment. Coach Nunnally thought the best coaches will make a second adjustment to your adjustment. Now it's my turn again to make my second adjustment.

I saw this firsthand when coaching in the NBA. There are so many decisions and subtle adjustments an NBA coach has to make in a single game. The obvious ones are changing defenses or making substitutions, but there are far more adjustments than those. We also have to adjust mindsets, just as managers and leaders must if they want to get the best out of their people.

In basketball, we may spend an entire time-out trying to get our guys to still believe we can win even though we are down eight with one minute left. We may have to get a player to continue shooting even though he is zero for nine that game. We may have to settle a player down because he had two bad fouls called on him. Coaching and leadership are every bit as much about resetting mindsets either for the individual or the entire team and organization as they are about making strategic adjustments.

One final thought: You have to have great eyes to see what you need to adjust. You have to have great ears to hear what you may need to adjust. You have to have a great mind to know what strategic adjustments you need to make. And when you make a difficult adjustment, you have to have the courage to stay with it and make it work.

HUMILITY

Humility is three things. It's an understanding that you're part of something much bigger and more important than yourself. It's the acknowledgement that you don't have all the answers and you're on the path towards improvement and growth. It's the awareness that following the necessary process is the only way to create the desired result and that process never truly ends.

SHAKA SMART, HEAD COACH, UNIVERSITY OF TEXAS

You may be wondering where I'm going with this word. To me, humility is a great separator when combined with everything else we have discussed. I believe humility can be present even if your position calls for you to demand things from others. Humility is how you carry yourself and does not have to be at odds with the position you hold, the responsibilities you have, or the pressure that may exist. You might be surprised to learn that humility is a trait that many of the great players in the NBA possess. In a world where you might anticipate

> *Humility is how you carry yourself and does not have to be at odds with the position you hold, the responsibilities you have, or the pressure that may exist.*

big egos, most players are humble.

It's often been said that true humility is not thinking less of yourself, it's thinking of yourself less. Where I also believe humility plays an integral part in individual and team success is that humility says: "I don't know it all. I do need to learn more. I am open and available to be taught." In other words, humility keeps us on that path of self-improvement that all greats travel.

Stan Van Gundy told me that the NBA puts everybody in check. He said: "This game humbles you. Every time you think you have all the answers, someone comes along and has better ones." I can also tell you from personal experience that just when you think you can't be beaten, the team that everyone knows you should beat shows up with their best game and beats you. Stan is right that in most competitive environments, sports or corporate, we all will be humbled at some point.

Are there coaches, leaders, and great athletes who may not see eye to eye with me on this? I would say there are some examples of this out there, but I will also argue that when humility is added to greatness *that* is when you have a special player, leader, or employee. That is the teammate everyone loves to play with. And when your best player is humble, that is when special things can happen for the team.

Tom Brady comes to mind in that he combines a humble attitude with an incredible talent and a powerful will to win. That combination makes him the teammate everyone wants to play with. But the separator is his humility, as most of the great pro athletes have the talent and the will. It's the humility that creates the "want" to play with him. Very few of his stature would look at themselves and say, "You are the worst quarterback in the game," as he has been known to say in practice after he did not execute up to his standards. We have heard Brady, in a postgame interview, say "Well, I really sucked today." He doesn't think he is God's gift to football—and that is what endears his teammates to him. (Let me state a personal note here: no matter what line of work we are in, none of us is "God's gift" to that office, that team, or to that game we play. In fact, the opposite is true: that office, that team, that game we play is God's gift to us!)

I saw humility in the very first meeting I was in with Steve Ballmer. The meeting was shortly after Steve took complete ownership of the Clippers. Doc Rivers, Dave Wohl, and I were there representing the team and the front office. We also had some players in town—Chris Paul, DeAndre Jordan, Blake Griffin, and Matt Barnes, and we all met for dinner at a restaurant in Beverly Hills. When Steve spoke up, he said, "I'm new at this. I don't know how to be an owner just yet. I am going to rely on all of you to help me learn as quickly as I can."

Steve had been the CEO at Microsoft before becoming owner of an NBA team in a major market, so he could have come in as if he knew everything. Instead, he led with humility. We left dinner thinking this was a leader we not only wanted to follow but also one we wanted to give our best to.

His kind of success and status could have led some in this new position to be cocky and arrogant, but Steve was nothing of the sort. He brought so much to the table and combined a humility with it that won us all over. Humility was the separator—not the wealth, the reputation, or the fact that he was a CEO.

As I have spoken around the country, I have been in conversations with many C-suite executives, and I can tell you that the great majority of leaders I have met have been humble. And as I observed their humility, I have seen that it is a major part of why their teams *want* to come to work each day rather than see themselves as *having to* come to work!

Finally, let me bring up Jay Wright, the head coach of the NCAA

Champion Villanova Wildcats. As Jay was preparing his team for a grueling NCAA tournament run, he also kept close tabs on one of his former assistants, Pat Chambers, the head coach of Penn State. Pat's team charted a course of their own through the NIT Tournament, which they eventually won.

You can imagine the time Jay spent preparing his team for their own run. I experienced it in the NBA finals, and trust me, you feel like every waking moment is directed at what you can do to put your team in the best position to win against the best teams out there. Nothing else enters your mind. But Jay found time at every stop Penn State made to communicate with Pat about what he saw and how proud he was. That is the unseen humility that makes Jay so good at what he does and makes so many quality players want to play for him. And, yes, he does look for that same trait in the players he recruits.

I offer two last reminders:

1. In all competitive fields you will be humbled, so don't get cocky!

2. Humility may not be a "must" to succeed at the highest levels of production or leadership, but it can be an incredible separator. I like to think of humility as being a leader's Velcro. It attracts people to you and keeps people attached!

You can be humble and confident, but I am not sure you can be humble and cocky. Cockiness erodes humility, confidence, and talented individuals. What I know for sure is this: the combination of humility and confidence is a championship formula!

INVESTMENT

We're not on this stage just because of talent
or ability. We're up here because of 4:00 a.m.;
because of two-a-days, or five-a-days.
We're up here because of a dream and let nothing
stand in our way. We were never satisfied.

KOBE BRYANT, NBA CHAMPION, LOS ANGELES LAKERS

Those who invest the most in their careers have a greater chance at success than those who don't. Simple? Yes. Do most people invest in their own development to the level of their goals and dreams? The answer is likely no. Everyone wants to win, but first you must make the commitment to what it takes to win: investment.

The best of the best invest. They invest monetarily. They invest by sacrificing. They invest by working harder and more often. They invest by expanding their knowledge. They invest by keeping their bodies in great shape. They invest by putting thought into planning strategy. They understand that success has a price, and that price is the investment you put in toward the goal you seek to attain.

Warren Buffet has been known to say, "Investing in yourself is the best thing you can do. Nobody can tax your investment in your talent or take it away from you." As I have shared with you, one of my own investments has been a commitment to reading two or more hours a day, every day, as a means to build my knowledge. To be the best, you have to invest. Jay Bilas says, "Hard work is not punishment. Hard work is the price of admission for the opportunity to reach sustained excellence." The right sacrifices have often turned into my most powerful investments.

I do think, however, that we are living in a time when investment is at risk of decay along with the rising tide of entitlement. We regularly hear complaints about the millennial generation's sense of entitlement, but let's not fool ourselves into thinking that entitlement is a characteristic that only the young possess. I have seen it in people who have been at a company for a long time and feel they are owed something simply because of their years of service. I like to look at it this way: your pay check is your responsibility, not your employer's.

Young people do have their own entitlement issues to overcome as well. For some who have experienced success early, easy, and often, they begin to think that such success is guaranteed, but when they take that step from college to a career, they fail to see that they become rookies again. They often forget about the work they had to put in to achieve whatever they achieved in the past. Or, in many instances, they came from systems where rewards were offered for minimal work and they grow to expect such rewards to continue. That can make it difficult for them to see that they will fail if they do not work and grow as they encounter more difficult challenges and higher standards.

Entitlement is the enemy of success as a team or for an individual no matter what age. It brings with it many team and individual killers: complacency, a weak work ethic, an "I'm-better" mentality— none of which can exist if growth, development, improvement, and success are the goal.

I believe we must constantly earn what we get regardless of age and regardless of history. In the world of professional sports, many young people—rookies—enter with a history of success. They have had great careers in college or high school and have been accustomed to being at the top of their competitive level. Obviously, if that wasn't the case, we would never see them have a shot at the NBA. But each new start puts them back into rookie status again. They have to again earn their status at the new level.

Just like several of the words we have already examined, like trust and respect, you must earn investment. You are not entitled to it.

You have to "earn the ask"

One of the mentors who invested in me was Hal Nunnally, a man for whom I had tremendous respect because he had such a strong value system. But Hal made me *earn* his investment in me. He tested me. He would give all the knowledge a person wanted, all the knowledge he had within him, but only if he knew you had worked for it. He had notebooks full of ideas and plays and notes he'd taken. I used to pester him to share his notebooks. "No, no," he'd say. "You need to ask me questions. The information in the notebooks will come out, but you have to ask me questions."

I thought about what he said and eventually came to understand what he was teaching me without saying so directly. *I had to earn the ask*! You're not just handed the knowledge. You don't just get the sale. You don't just get his notebook. I had to earn the ask. And I earned it through showing up at his office. I earned it through reading his basketball magazines—not his notebooks because I knew I couldn't get there yet. I earned it by asking questions. I earned it by listening to him talk, by watching him coach. Eventually I earned the ask. I got the notebooks.

A salesperson has to invest in the potential client. She has to invest her time. He has to invest his care. He has to invest his concern.

She has to invest her transfer of knowledge to that person she's trying to sell. And that's what we have to do in all relationships, whether in sales, coaching, or leadership. We have to earn the ask.

Earning the ask is the opposite of feeling entitled. And the entitlement/investment struggle holds just as true for teams as it does for individuals. Teams can't expect their paths to be easier because they are supposed to be good or because they are ranked or because everyone says they have a lot of talent.

If you don't take anything else away from this book, take this: Teams of entitlement never win titles!

I think this applies to both sports and business. Entitlement may feel easier at the time, but investment is what works best over time. Just like with our money, we earn and then we invest. We invest and then it grows. That same concept holds true for our improvement and success! Just as with many of the all-stars you have been introduced to in this book, it has often taken them ten to fifteen years of hard work to become "overnight sensations." What they all have in common is that they made the decision to invest.

TALENT

T alent alone does not win championships, create a great sales force, or make a person great. Talent is part of success, as you have to have some level of talent to have a chance to reach the highest levels of any competitive environment. But there are teams and organizations out there that have talent and never win. Professional teams in all sports have talent. We could name a number of teams that had a lot of talent yet did not win much and certainly did not win up to the level their talent would suggest they should.

The way I see it, there are players who have *talent* and there are *talented* players. I will say that again. There are players with talent and there are talented players. What's the difference?

If you study both words, *talent* and *talented*, the difference is small, but the results are enormous. The difference is two letters; talented has an E and a D at the end. In my world, ED stands for "extra dimension." I'm talking about the extra dimension that each of the talented players brings to their team, their individual game, and to *the* game. If you asked championship coaches which player they would rather have, they would go for the talented player. The great teams do not want the players with just talent. They want talented players.

That extra dimension shows up in different ways. For Peyton Manning, it shows up in his incredible preparation discipline, giving his team confidence that as their leader, he will always be the most prepared. They know his preparation will provide him the poise they all need when the game is on the line.

For Kevin Garnett, his extra dimension was his passion and ability to energize the team. For Paul Pierce it was his availability; he seldom missed a game or practice. The common thought in professional sports is that one "bility" is most important and a key separator for greatness: *availability*. It's the same in the workplace. If your best salespeople call in sick or don't commit to their sales calls with enthusiasm, what good are they to you that day? Availability means bringing your best self, your best mind, and your best spirit every day regardless of circumstance.

Being a talented player means you bring something to the team above and beyond your talent alone. As Doc Rivers used to say around playoff time: "Every team knows your strength as a player. When they take that away, how else can you help this team win a championship?" What is that extra dimension you can bring to your team? If the answer is nothing else, then your value is limited when it's crunch time.

> *Championship talent goes beyond what you do well. It's what you can do well when what you do well isn't going well.*

Championship talent goes beyond what you do well. It's what you can do well when what you do well isn't going well. The mother of Ronda Rousey, the former UFC champion, always said to her, "You're not training to be the best in the world, you're training to be the best in the world on your worst day." Become that talented player, not just the player who has talent!

CHAPTER 3

The Champion's Compass

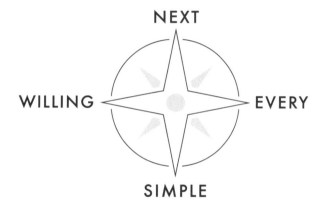

NEXT

WILLING   EVERY

SIMPLE

Doc shared a great statement with me at the end of our third season coaching the Los Angeles Clippers. We'd had three very good regular seasons, winning more than fifty games in each, but a good regular-season team was not his aspiration for any of us. For him, good enough was never a goal. Pretty good was never a strategy.

In his mind, "We had done a lot of winning but never were the *winner*." This tells you Doc's mindset. He coaches to become the world champion, and every day is centered on how we can get the team to that level. This is a characteristic of all successful people. Succeeding is not about doing a good job, it's all about doing your *best* job.

In those first three years with the Clippers, we never became "the winner." So, I began to do a lot of thinking, reading, and talking to those who had ascended to the "winners" level about why others won a title and we did not. I needed to find out how they reached champion status. And selfishly, I wanted to figure what we were missing. What were we not doing? What were we not paying attention to? What did we need to incorporate that we hadn't?

I also thought back and evaluated why and how our Boston Celtics team won the title in 2008. There had to be something that became the separator other than luck (although don't fool yourself, luck does play a part in becoming a champion. It's not the key factor, but every winner usually experiences some).

After months of thought, study, and analysis, I concluded that the teams that made it to the finals —and for that matter the teams that made it to their conference finals—had a number of things in common on the floor. They all had good talent. They all passed the ball well. They all played hard. They all played as a team. They all competed on defense. Many of their strengths from a tactical and physical standpoint were similar, but there were differences that each of *the winners* possessed from a mental standpoint. These mental separators allowed them to persevere through eight preseason games, eighty-two regular season games, and four competitive playoff rounds to determine who ultimately would be the champions.

I call this separator "The Champion's Compass." Just as a compass provides us direction and keeps us moving toward our desired destination, giving us a way to get back on track when we veer off course, so too does the Champion's Compass provide direction for teams. The teams that are mentally tough enough and buy into these mindsets are the ones that have the best chance of creating the separation needed to give themselves a much-needed advantage.

So, what separates those who do a lot of winning and those who are *the* winners?

NEXT

No matter what happens to us, we have to move on to the next play, the next challenge, the next day, the next project. Whether we experience failure or success as a team or personally, we have to move on to the next thing. Success

> *I call this separator "The Champion's Compass." Just as a compass provides us direction and keeps us moving toward our desired destination, giving us a way to get back on track when we veer off course, so too does the Champion's Compass provide direction for teams.*

has many tests, and one of them is failure. Can you learn and move on from failure? Can you learn and move on after success? Can you move on to the next step?

Next also applies to winners who are able to take their game to the next level: next-level effort, preparation, focus, discipline, and thinking.

From a team standpoint, we find that the best—the strongest teams and the most resilient teams—are that way because of the belief they have in their teammates, those next to them in the trenches. Or as they often say in the special ops world: I know I can always count on the guy next to me.

Finally, it has been my experience that the best learn to take two or three "next steps" each season to get to that "next level." It can be the next step in their execution or the next step in their effort. It might be the next step in how they handle adversity with more maturity. Every champion must take that next step on the climb.

Staying the same is the enemy of next.

SIMPLE

Recall the philosophy I mentioned in the beginning of this book: success lies in simplicity; confusion lives in sophistication.

The simple things become big things when the competition is the stiffest. It goes without saying that when you compete against the best, execution becomes one of the difference makers. Execution is all about the little things, the simple things.

After every game we played, I gave Doc my game notes. These included positive things we did and needed to continue to do, and the things we did not execute as well and needed to correct. I also focused on messages we could send to the team the next day about the good and bad I had observed.

During one stretch of games, as a staff we kept talking about how we were not paying attention to the little things. It could be we did not block-out, and the opponent scored off an offensive rebound. It could be that we did not get into help position on defense and we gave the opponent a free driving lane to the basket or that we did not rotate on defense based on the play the opponent just ran.

Each one of these was a fundamental and simple action we worked on almost every day. Each of these plays was an isolated possession and did not seem to have an impact on the outcome at that moment of the game. It could have been a simple mistake in the first minute. At the time, it did not seem to have any significance in the game. It could be the ninth possession of the first quarter, and again it might seem to have no immediate significance. Then on the eighth possession of the second quarter and fourth possession of the third quarter we repeat a simple mistake. At the time, in isolation, these simple things do not appear to have an impact.

I decided we needed to show the team the impact each of these "insignificant," simple possessions actually had on the game. I charted every *simple mistake* that took away the opportunity to score and provided the opponent a scoring opportunity on their next possession. The number of points the opponent scored off the "little things" was an eye opener for all of us. We gave up thirty-two points on little things—those things that did not appear to be important back in the first quarter or first half.

The lesson is that everything counts once the final buzzer sounds. Simple wins a lot more games than spectacular ever will!

EVERY

Every second of every minute of every quarter of every game, by everybody, every time out, every night, in every arena. Teams that take plays off significantly reduce their chances of becoming champions. Those lapses of a few possessions or a few minutes build up over the course of a game and come back to be the deciding factor in winning or losing.

Every also becomes critically important when a game, a season, a huge client's sales pitch, or a marketing mistake ends in a loss. I like to say: every day counts on the last day!

After our postgame championship celebration in 2008, when most everyone had already left the Boston Garden, the coaches and their families remained. Deep in the arena, in the office the assistants used for pregame preparation, we were there talking about what we had just accomplished: winning an NBA title. Everything was positive, and we were filled with humility and gratitude as we rehashed the series, the playoffs, and the season. It was total satisfaction and a feeling of a job well done.

Now let's fast-forward two years to the 2010 NBA finals when we lost to the Los Angeles Lakers in their arena. I vividly remember the coaches' locker room after that loss. After several minutes of complete silence, the talk began. "We should have done this in the third quarter. We should have worked this player harder to keep him in better shape during the year." We commiserated, "If only we could have done this in game three." The talk was entirely different but provided a great lesson about the word "every." When you get to the end, and you lose a game, a sale, or a client, you look back on all the days you put in and the decisions you made leading up to the final horn, and it teaches you a great lesson that all champions have figured out: Every day counts when it's the last day!

Had we focused on every little decision and every simple possession at the time it occurred, we may very well have been the NBA Champions again in 2010. Every one of those days and decisions really counted when we looked back on them. And we found out too late: when the season ended—and we lost. Take care of every day every day!

WILLING

Everyone who aspires to greatness has to be willing to be teachable and coachable. Winners are open minded. They want to learn new things. They want to grow. They are willing to play for the *team* and not for themselves, to play *for* a teammate not just with a teammate.

The biggest "willings" for improvement and accomplishing our goals are:

- Willing to listen.
- Willing to work.
- Willing to learn.
- Willing to be a great teammate.
- Willing to change.

The Champion's Compass is powerful! The team that may best exemplify the Champion's Compass is the New England Patriots in the 2017 Super Bowl. They were down 28–3 in the third quarter. There was never any turning on each other or tuning each other out. Entering the fourth quarter, things did not look good in the eyes of Patriot fans. But the only eyes that counted that day were the eyes of the Patriots' staff and players. They kept getting to the *next* play and putting all they had practiced and prepared for into *every* snap. They stayed focused and continued to take care of the *simple* things that each task called for. They never panicked. And finally, just as they have built their team all year, they were all *willing* to keep executing their roles, doing their jobs, trusting the system and process, and listening to their coaches and to one another. No one got *into* themselves. They stayed *in the team.*

They epitomized the power of the Champion's Compass!

CHAPTER 4

Success Triangles:
The Power Thoughts
of Champions

1. THREE GAPS

2. THREE DIMENSIONS
    OF SUCCESS

3. THREE SETS

4. THREE C'S

5. THREE BESTS

6. THREE DON'TS

7. THREE BATTLES

8. THREE INGREDIENTS

9. THREE INS

10. THREE UPS

T alk to an engineer about strength in structural support, and you are likely to get a treatise on the triangle. Talk to a basketball coach about movement, and you're likely to get endless discussion about the role of triangles in ball movement, player movement, player spacing, defensive schemes, and shutting down passing lanes, just to name a few.

Play for that same coach, and he or she is likely to shout instructions to you in nice, tidy, memorable refrains of three. Scientists will tell us that the average person may only be able to hold three or four things in mind at once. I have always believed that breaking things into manageable thirds can make complex concepts seem simple, memorable, and actionable.

This chapter explores some of the concepts—the "success triangles"—that I have formulated by working with championship-caliber people and that, working in concert with many of the words, form the core of this book.

THREE GAPS
CAPABILITY, KNOWLEDGE, AND TEAM-NESS

It is my belief that we all have more in us as leaders, as coaches, as players, and as people. To get the most out of ourselves, it's a constant exercise in self-awareness, recognition, and learning. We have to recognize the gap between where we are today and where we want to go. Once we recognize that gap, we must then spend time learning how we can fill it. The three gaps we must fill are:

TEAM-NESS GAP

Capability Gap

No matter who we are, how old we are, or what line of work we are in, we have all accomplished a certain amount in our lives, and we should be proud of those accomplishments. But success is not about what you have accomplished, it's what you *should have accomplished* with the talent that you possess. If we are truthful with ourselves, we will see that there is a gap between the two. This is the Capability Gap.

When I am introduced before a speech, I always tell the audience that I love being introduced. I know the majority are thinking that I must be egotistical. But I explain that it has nothing to do with ego;

it has everything to do with education. Introductions remind me of a lifelong lesson that all successful people, teams, and organizations live by. You see, when the person tells the audience where I have been and what I have done, I am reminded of two very important questions:

- Where am I capable of going?

- What am I capable of becoming?

I am proud of my accomplishments, but I'm focused on how much more I can get out of myself to maximize my talent and potential.

We all have this gap. Those of us who strive to fill it are the ones who have the best chance to get to where we want to go and become what we dream of becoming. That's why we see and read about the great athletes and how they continue to work on their craft even when others think, "That's enough for me today." The best of the best understand that they have more in them. They are on a never-ending mission to fill their Capability Gap.

The best among us understand that accomplishment is about where we have been. *Becoming* is all about where we can go and how much better we can be. The choice is simple to explain but tough to execute. You can live in the past or you can work to make your future the best that you can make it.

Knowledge Gap

We all have a certain amount of knowledge that we have acquired during our lives. Whatever that is, it's not enough to keep up in this ever-changing world. We can't keep up, let alone get ahead, without continuing to build our knowledge bank.

I believe that the more you know about your craft, the better chance you have to be successful. For athletes, it could be knowing more about the positions they play. For a trainer, it could be knowing more about safe and speedy injury recovery. For a coach, it could be learning more about a defensive scheme or studying film on how to contain a great player. For a leader, it could be learning about how to deal with a talented employee who does not contribute to the team. Or it could simply be learning what the "nexts" might be in your industry.

All of this is an exercise in knowledge acquisition, learning more about all things that pertain to your life and career. You would not have reached your current position without some level of knowledge, but the knowledge of today does not always determine the success of tomorrow.

George Raveling always told me that at Nike they wanted to "get to the future first." In order to accomplish that, they have to envision what the future may look like and be prepared. The same holds true for any industry. For those who think they will fail if they don't get to the future first, I would add this to Nike's mantra: "If you can't get to the future first, then get there second ... but better." You may not have been first to market or the first coach to come up with a defensive scheme, but that doesn't mean you can't learn from how the first did it and devise a way to do it better.

What matters most is not what you know, it's what you need to know to get to where you want to go in your life and career. It's about filling that Knowledge Gap!

Team-ness Gap

Going back to that first September team meeting where I started this book, the word that resonated the most was "team!" And why does this resonate so often and so powerfully? Because it's more than just a word to any group that wants to become a collection of team members willing to sacrifice for one another. That's when you have a true team!

So many people simply do not know the true definition of a team. Many will say it's a group that wears the same uniform. Or it's a group that works on the same floor of an office building. Or it's a division of a company. A team is more than those who work together, those who play together, or those who work in the same office. I can tell a true team by watching them and seeing whether or not there is a "team-ness" about them.

I first heard this word "team-ness" from Shaka Smart, now (2018) the head basketball coach at the University of Texas. Just like many words or phrases, it stuck with me, but I had yet to fully understand it.

The more I studied championship teams, the more I saw that this team-ness became the trait that all championship groups embodied. It was an air they had that told you they were together. It was present in everything they did. As I put more thought to this, I determined that team-ness is comprised of three parts:

- Teammate
- Teamwork
- Team

TEAMMATE A teammate is more than that guy next to you. It is more than someone you practice with and more than those who share the locker room. Being a teammate means you have one, and only one, agenda: a team agenda. There can be no personal agendas on a championship team. A teammate is someone who is *over himself* and *into the team*. Being a teammate is immersing ourselves in doing everything we can to help the team and our teammates succeed while knowing that we will get the same in return.

The key part of being a teammate is understanding and accepting your role. In order for a team to win, it has to use the strengths that it has in each of its members. Each role is not created equal. On great teams, roles are defined by what you do best for the team. Whether the player accepts it, understands it, and executes his role will be the difference in success or failure.

It's not easy to accept a role that might be different from the one you want or think you are worthy of. On our teams, we talked to our players about

- being an all-star at your role,
- understanding the role we need from you for us to win a championship, and
- understanding your role is the value you bring to the team.

This approach to roles flourished with that 2008 Celtics team. Earlier in the book, I mentioned the sacrifice the Big Three—Paul Pierce, Ray Allen, and Kevin Garnett—made in terms of sharing offensive roles. They all understood and accepted an offense that did not feature any individual as our only go-to guy.

I saw something similar play out when the media and fans saw Kevin Garnett as the savior. It would be Kevin's team according to them.

Not so fast.

Kevin made it known from day one that "This is Paul's team. He's been here. He's put in the time." Instantly we had the best example we could that this year was going to be the "year of the teammate" and the "year of sacrifice" in Boston.

Kevin even went so far as to make sure Paul was still introduced last in pregame introductions, which in the NBA is known as a sign of respect. It was a visible sign to all on the team that Kevin was willing to sacrifice his personal glory for improving the strength of team. But in all honesty, Kevin thinks differently than most players. To him this wasn't a sacrifice. This was simply what a teammate does! Kevin would not accept any interviews unless Paul and Ray were included. That is a player who is "over himself." That is a true teammate.

TEAMWORK When I think of teamwork I think of a concept originating in Southern Africa—Ubuntu. Doc brought Ubuntu to our team before the 2007/2008 season. It is a word that means "humanity." The literal translation is, "I am because we are." At its core are two basic tenets:

- People are people because of other people.
- I can only be all I can be if you are all you can be.

Ubuntu is all about the other guy, not about me. I become my best me when others become their best me. That's its beauty. We all must work with each other, and more importantly, for each other in order to bring out the best in each other.

The only way a team can work is if teammates work together. There are many examples of teams in all sports that have a lot of talent yet never win championships. Often, they are filled with players focused on getting their stats. They are players satisfied with personal attention, even after a loss, players who "use" their teammates rather than "work with" their teammates. Teamwork is just not important to them, and they ultimately find out that winning really isn't, either.

Ubuntu is about an understanding that a player cannot be his best unless his teammates are at their best. And the only way to do that is to help the other players be their best. Because at its core Ubuntu is all about sacrifice, Ubuntu rewards those who engage in a teamwork approach. "Teamwork teams" are the ones always left standing in the end.

Champions are formed when a coaching staff finds the players they need and defines the roles for each player. Then it's the players who take over and make sure they integrate their roles into the whole, knowing that if they are missing one role, they are playing at a deficit. They know it is on them to make the parts work together. They know for the team to work it starts with teamwork!

TEAM The second part of the Ubuntu philosophy: "I can only be all I can be if you are all you can be," speaks to the concept of jealousy. It means that I need you to be at your best so that I will be at my best. On that Celtics team, it meant for Ray Allen to be at his best—shooting the ball—he needed Rajon Rondo to be at his best—penetrating the defense to open Ray's shot. By Rajon doing what he did best and not worrying about doing anything else, it allowed Ray to do what he did best. Rajon created the environment for Ray to flourish, and he had to do this and not be worried about who got the credit.

This is playing without jealousy. The best companies are the ones that have jealousy-free cultures. Without necessarily knowing the word, they are organizations that live the Ubuntu philosophy.

Just because you wear the same jersey or the same company logo, you're not automatically a team. Until you are willing to sacrifice yourself for the betterment of the group, you will be just a group of individuals who dress alike.

THREE DIMENSIONS OF SUCCESS

YESTERDAY, TODAY, TOMORROW

I am often asked this question when I talk about the "Three Gaps" we discussed earlier: "The Three Gaps all seem to be centered on the future. So, do you not pay any attention to the past?"

This is a great question, one that is important to the success of a team, organization, or any individual. It's not the future alone that allows us the best chance at success. The future is what's next while the past is all about how we arrived where we are. The present is what we are doing to ensure the future we want.

In order to make sure we get the most out of all that has happened in the past and apply it to what we want to happen in the future, I look at it like this, through what I call, "The Three Dimensions of Success." We have to

learn from the past,

produce in the present, and

prepare for the future.

We have to *learn from* the past not *live in* the past!

It is very important that we learn from what happened in the past but equally important that we don't live in the past. Regardless of how good quarter one was we are now in quarter two. Regardless of how many points you scored last game or last quarter there is still the next game or the next quarter.

When we live in the past, we lose the edge we need for the present. And if we don't take care of the present, it will have a negative impact on our future. Those who live in the past often do not have the urgency needed to succeed. We must be aware of failure but not live in the past. Failure is so personal that it can be hard to move on from it.

In a team setting, we must not let failures or losses linger in the locker room. Locker rooms where those things linger are locker rooms that lose. Locker rooms that learn are locker rooms that have the best chance of rebounding from setbacks. Learning locker rooms understand the importance of leadership, and leaders are needed most when the losses begin to build.

We have to *produce* in the present, not *coast* in the present!

Just because we had success in the past, it doesn't guarantee success in the present. The past represents the lessons we have learned. The present offers the tests we must face. Producing in the present is all about executing your role in your organization to the best of your ability. Success does not allow a day of coasting or a day of living off yesterday's success. Success requires a daily approach. It is not a "when you want to" proposition. Success is a series of tests followed by lessons leading up to the next test. And the cycle continues.

Producing in the present is all about executing the role you have been given to the best of your ability each day. To the public you may be invisible, but to the team you are invaluable! And it's usually the invisible players who provide a significant difference when you analyze championship teams.

Role players—those invisible ones—have to trust in their leadership. The best leaders see the invisible and value their contributions. Do your job to the best of your ability, and trust that your leaders will see it, reward it, and maybe even expand it as time moves on.

But also understand the promotion or expanded role is not automatic. You can be great at your role but if that is all you can offer, chances are you will have to stay in that role. If you want to expand your role, you must use the off season or the nights and weekends to study, work on, and perfect something else that adds value to the team.

We have to *prepare* for the future, not *wish for* the future!

While we take lessons from the past and work to produce in the present, this is all part of *preparing* for the future. Preparation is a critical word when it comes to success. If we are not prepared for what is about to happen or what we are about to do, we will always be playing from behind and reacting. Remember the definition for preparation that was provided earlier: Be there before you get there.

Lawrence Frank, former NBA head coach and current (2018) president of basketball operations for the Los Angeles Clippers likes to say: "The best coaches and leaders have to have the answers before they ask the questions." This is what the best of the best do. They prepare to the degree that they're ready for all situations. They have researched the competition. They have practiced their presentation. They have thought of all the questions that might be asked. They have pictured the environment in their minds before they arrive. They try to *be there before they get there.*

As we look at these three time frames—past, present, and future—let's put them in the context of what I call the "Three Most Important Days":

- Yesterday
- Today
- Tomorrow

Why are these three days so important?

- *Yesterday* **is all about** *evaluation* **and** *education.* What did we do? What did we learn? What can we take from it?

- *Today* **is all about** *execution*, making sure we do our jobs and execute our roles as well as we can in this moment.

- *Tomorrow* **is all about** *preparation*, making sure we are not just ready for tomorrow but *prepared* for tomorrow. The difference? Ready is being there and doing what is asked of me. Prepared says: I have thought about this. I have researched. I have practiced. I won't just be there. I will bring my best because I know what is expected of me. I will deliver my best.

There is a power in each of these three days that can move us forward and keep us on our path for success.

THREE SETS

SKILL SET, MINDSET, RESET

There are three sets we must master if we want have a chance to reach our goals:

Skill Set

Skill set applies to whatever skills one has to master to be successful at his or her craft. This set is on each of us as individuals. We must find out what those skills are and then put a plan together to master them. Whatever mastery takes in terms of effort, time, and repetition, we have to put into our plan.

Mindset

Best-selling author, Jon Gordon, spoke to our LA Clippers front-office team, and he mentioned something that has stuck with me ever since. While talking about the ingredients of championship organizations, he said teams "win in the mind first." Getting their mind right (their "mindset") is first and foremost.

The mind is powerful in terms of our confidence and our belief, and, in turn, how we transmit that confidence and belief to the rest of our team. With each new day I can bring any attitude I want to the workday, to the office, and to my teammates. I can provide energy or I can suck the energy out of the building. I can come with a focus and determination that will not only help me but also carry over to the team. At game time I can arrive to compete and win rather than to serve my own ego.

How we set our mind often sets our day. And the power of an attitude is that it can spread—good and bad. Winners find a way to spread positivity, energy, and teamwork. They can snap a teammate out of a funk. The mindset you have for yourself, if positive and "we" oriented, becomes a force multiplier for everyone you come in contact with each day.

Reset

We must learn to reset ourselves after a mistake or after failure. One thing is for sure, we will experience both, no matter how good our team is or how good we are. Failure and mistakes are part of any competitive environment. Basketball is not a game of perfect. Leadership is not a game of perfect. Life is not a game of perfect. As is often said in the NBA, every team has issues, but the winners get through them and past them. The ability to reset yourself or your team afterward is the key to becoming successful.

What the best of the best say is: "Mistakes are going to be made; just make sure they're new ones."

If I make the same mistake over and over again—or if I make too many new mistakes—I should be taken out of the game. But the fact remains that mistakes will happen, and we have to learn from them and work hard not to repeat them. So often we so fear the consequence of failure that it keeps us from even starting. And I think we all would agree that we can't reap the benefits of something that we never start. We can't become what we have always dreamed of becoming if we never start. We can't fear the consequence of failing to the point that we never start. Part of starting is accepting that mistakes will happen. Will you learn from them?

We are accustomed to hearing people talk about the value of risk-taking and being placed in positions beyond our comfort zones. And maybe the prospect of coaching in the NBA was both of those for me, but in my mind accepting the position was about the challenge of growing and of seeing if I could do it. That kept me going on those days when I knew I had to get better. I just made sure that once I reset my mindset I was going to keep it that way. I refused to focus on failure. It was all about challenging my capability level!

THREE C'S

OVERCOMING COMPLACENCY, CONCEIT, AND COMPROMISE

When thinking about the upcoming year, it's easy to center on the toughest teams on your schedule and the difficult matchups you will have with the best players in your league. This is similar to how corporations must enter each new fiscal year focused on their biggest competitors and changing market trends. There is value to thinking about your toughest competition and giving them concerted thought, detailed planning, and smart strategy. But there's another opponent we may not think about or prepare for, an opponent who dresses in our own locker rooms and wears our own uniform. Human nature.

When I coached the Boston Celtics or the Los Angeles Clippers, our toughest opponents weren't the Golden State Warriors, the San Antonio Spurs, or the Cleveland Cavaliers. More often than not, our greater opponent was human nature and how it affected our players throughout the course of a season.

I have seen many times when human nature kept a team from getting the most out of themselves or caused an individual to play selfishly. There is a basic instinct to look out for oneself. I have seen human nature manifest itself when we are asked to do something that takes us out of our comfort zone—when our instincts tell us to protect ourselves and hold back so we won't be embarrassed or fail. And human nature reveals itself in the fight or flight instinct. When things become difficult, some dig down and play harder while others quit.

We must prepare ourselves to battle these aspects of human nature as intentionally as we prepare for a tough opponent or a difficult part of our schedule. Human nature can reveal itself in self-preservation and selfishness, and as we all know, these instincts can kill a team.

Pat Riley, one of the greatest coaches of all time, had a saying that gets to the heart of how human nature can affect a team. He called it the "disease of me"—worrying about me first, protecting my brand, making sure I get my recognition. In essence it's creating a personal agenda vs a team-first agenda.

Championship teams will tell you that you can only have one agenda, and that agenda is to win. This agenda has no place within it for personal agendas and no time for players to give in to human nature at every tough turn, every bad game, or any personal setback.

Just like the rosters that are filled with the toughest players on their respective teams, human nature has two very tough players as well: success and failure.

Success

Achieving success is always a great feeling. It's tangible proof that what you did and the work you put in actually did pay off. While it is a great feeling, once you accomplish it success can also lead to certain attitudes that will ultimately bring you down. Three of the most devastating are:

- **Complacency** (I don't have to work that hard or work right now.)
- **Conceit** (I did it last year—I'm good—I've already proven myself.)
- **Compromise** (I can take this play off; I can turn it on anytime.)

COMPROMISE

Complacency is that feeling of "we got this;" we don't have to work as hard because we know how to win. We can always get to it, but don't need to right now. We can cruise now and turn it on when we need it. We've proven we can win and we know what to do.

Conceit is the opposite of humility. You think you are the team's gift, that you are the one they all know they need to be successful. The ultimate form of conceit in basketball is when you say you are God's gift to the game. The player with humility would have said basketball is God's gift to me.

Compromise is when we feel that maybe we can skip this step or not work as hard today because we know we can always turn it on. I can always cram as time gets close. All of these are exercises in compromising the very things that made us successful. We are compromising our preparation, our process, our work ethic.

All three mindsets are destructive to a team. Complacency will be tested and most often will fail. Conceit leads to friction within the team, as the team members often cannot stand to play with this type of player. And compromise leads us down the path of taking short cuts or doing something that we normally wouldn't do, thinking we can always get back on track.

Here are some other thoughts that may help you as you look at the success you have had or the success you hope to achieve:

- **Behind any success is every day.** Success is not a one-time effort. It is the result of repeated efforts every day over a long period of time.

- **Success is not a game of perfect.** There will be mistakes and failures along the way. Understand that these happen to everyone who has become successful.

- **Success is not a game of genius.** Success does not require you to be the smartest person in the room. Success is more about the consistent work you put in.

- **Success is a battle against human nature.** The biggest waste of talent is when talent settles.

- **Success is about discipline.** It's comprised, as thought leader Jim Rohn taught me, of a few simple disciplines done every day; it is not a secret sauce.

- **Success is about self-evaluation.** There's a lot of con in this world, but the one person you can never con is yourself. You must evaluate yourself as truthfully as you can. Do a deep dive into YOU!

- **Success doesn't stop once you get there.** Michael Jordan said this. None of us (team or individual) has arrived. We may have reached a certain level of success. But we are not done. We have not arrived. It's not about what we've accomplished as much as it is what we accomplished relative to what we are capable of accomplishing.

- **Success requires a choice.** Are you interested, or are you committed?

- **Success should never be about money.** I have always believed that your paycheck is your responsibility, not your employer's. If you are good enough and if you bring enough value to your organization, the money will find you.

- **Success leaves footprints.** As we will discuss later in this chapter, you have to find them, follow them, and fit them.

- **Success requires stamina, discipline, and grind:**
  - *Improvement Stamina:* this is about understanding that success is often incremental, and you have to stick with it no matter how slow improvement seems.
  - *Development Discipline:* this is the resolve to keep getting better. There will be roadblocks along the way. There will be days when you may not feel like working and there will be days when it will seem like you are far away from where you want to be. You have to discipline yourself to overcome setbacks.
  - *Greatness Grind:* I often read about people who are considered to be at the top of their industry. We see these people once they have arrived at that point of distinction, but seldom do we see them on their way up. The journey is where the true magic happens. That is where they become who they are. That is where we would witness the day-to-day, week-to-week, month-to-month grind they put in to reaching success.

- **Success requires your all.** You must put your entire heart into something knowing it may be broken. Success is never guaranteed. The only guarantee success will give us is the guarantee that if we don't try we have no shot.

- **Success requires you to stop waiting**. The longer you wait, the less likely you will take action. We all know about the "Law of Diminishing Intent." The longer you "intend" to do something and never get around to it, the more you will guarantee that you are unlikely to achieve it.

- **Success very rarely occurs in a vacuum**. This is all about the importance of team. We all need others to help us achieve at our highest levels. Success is not a solo game.

- **Success, in its simplest form, is a result of**
  - the choices we make,
  - the actions we take, and
  - the circles we travel in.

Failure

Failure is such a personal hit to our ego ... unless you reset how we look at it. None of us want to experience it, but all of us will. As many people say, you have to fail before you can succeed. I understand what they are trying to convey here, but I look at it differently. I see failure as being part of the process of success if, and only if, you learn from it. If it's just something bad that happens to you and you do nothing about it, I don't see where that helps at all.

Many of us fail to understand just how smart success is. It's not going to let us achieve it just because we try it. Success will test us, and its biggest tests are failure and embarrassment. It wants to see how we react to each. Some of us are devastated when we fail while others are just embarrassed. Both reactions are why success puts these tests in front of us: to see how we react.

The best athletes, coaches, leaders, teams, and organizations all understand that these tests will be given. They understand that how we react to the tests determines a lot about our chance for success. The best of the best react the way champions react. You can treat failure as a *devastation* or an *education*. You either live with it or learn from it. The best learn from it. That doesn't mean they like it or hope it happens, they just know it *will* happen and they will get the most from it. In contrast, losers let failure take everything; it devastates them.

Embarrassment is a natural reaction because it does sting when we fail. But the best of the best understand that failure is what happens to us, it's not who we are. The only way it does that is if we continue to fail for the same reasons. When that's the case, I think everyone would say we deserve it.

The way you look at failure will influence the way you react to failure, and the way you react to failure is the way you will move on from failure. Too many of us keep ourselves from even trying because we fear the consequences. I encourage you to turn your mindset around. Again—what happens if you try AND IT WORKS!

My career in the NBA is a prime example. I had left college coaching and was enjoying a nice life running my own basketball camps. But then an opportunity came when Doc Rivers asked me if I would join his Celtics coaching staff. I have to tell you, I was honored to be asked but also had a little fear as to whether I would be good enough. I knew the NBA featured the best players in the world and within that group, some all-time greats. Any coach wants to coach great players, but what people don't know is that the best in the world want the best in the world coaching them. You need to know your stuff. If you don't and they see that seed of doubt in your eyes, they may shut you off and not listen to you. The NBA is a great league to work in, but it is also a very unforgiving and demanding league. So naturally I had doubts.

Luckily, I had this philosophy of TRY. What would happen if

I didn't do it? Sure, it would be hard, and sure, I had to study my tail off to catch up to all the great coaches Doc would hire, but what would happen if IT WORKED? And, man, did it work. We won an NBA World Championship. And we coached two NBA all-star games in 2008 and 2010.

In addition to my own thirst to keep learning, I was challenged to continue to improve to keep up with the rest of the staff, and especially with Doc and his knowledge of the game. Accepting Doc's offer taught me a great lesson—that sometimes you have to raise your game just to stay in the game. That was what the NBA did for me. I loved the everyday challenge of raising my game.

If I only feared the consequence of failing, I never would have been able to experience what being the best at what you do is all about or what success truly demands.

So, I ask you, if you knew it would work and you didn't try, how would that make you feel? That would be a regret that no one would want to have. Take it from someone who has faced such a decision and knows many in sports who have been there as well. Eliminate as many regrets as you can. Most important, work toward eliminating that fear of failure.

THREE BESTS

THE BEST, MY BEST, OUR BEST

THE BEST

MY BEST

OUR BEST

We hear the word "best" so often. Do we throw that term out too often and too loosely?

I often encounter people who are pressured to become the best at what they do, and they succumb to that pressure. They live in a world of constant frustration, hesitancy, and doubt. The task of being "the best" at what they do is daunting for them. It's not a character flaw. I think this is how most people are wired.

When speaking to sports or corporate teams, I often ask the audience, "Who is the best current player in the NBA?" I usually hear the same names: Lebron James, Steph Curry, Kevin Durant, Kawhi Leonard, Russell Westbrook, or James Harden. There's no question that these six deserve to be in the conversation, though we all might add another name or two. But for the sake of argument, let's say these six and these six only make our list.

There are 450 players in the NBA, so that means only six out of 450 have chance to be in the discussion for "the best." That means 444 players will not be in the running. Does that mean they should go find another profession? Of course not.

What people don't realize is that the NBA is made up of many more "role" players than "stars." So, it can become a daunting task to demand of someone that they be "the best."

There are two "bests" in the NBA (and for that matter two bests in any line of work):

- Those who are *the* best

- Those who have figured out how to become *my* best

The NBA is filled with players who have figured out how to become "my" best. They understand that to become "my" best is every bit as important to the team as it is to their careers.

How do you become "my" best? There are five key concepts to understand in order to reach "the best" or "my best":

1. **To be the best you have to beat the best at their best**. Becoming the best or becoming "my" best is about competition. You must be willing to compete.

2. **To be the best you have to bring your best every day**. Success resides in accountability. People operate either on an accountability track or a blame track. The best always live in the world of personal accountability.

3. **To be the best you have to learn the best from the best**. You must be a lifelong learner. Those six players we listed as being the best in the NBA are all constantly on a seek-and-find mission to improve, develop, and grow. They understand that they do not know it all but do have to learn it all. They are sponges when it comes to the things that can make them better players. "Learn-it-alls" fill the rosters of championship teams and senior corporate suites.

4. **To be the best you must demand the best from each other.** This pertains to people who work in a team setting, which is just about all of us. The best teams are the ones that are willing to push and be pushed by one another.

5. **The best are the best for a reason.** We have to go out and find out what those reasons are. In a world with so much access to information, there is no excuse for not finding out what made someone else successful. It is incumbent on us to find those reasons. We must learn to ask the questions that will elicit the information we need.

What you will learn on your way to becoming *the* best, is that you must give *my* best, and then as a team we become *our* best!

THREE DON'TS

DO NOT DISMISS
OBVIOUS, AGE, AND IDEAS

I often watch other people dismiss new ideas or ideas from another's perspective, and I cannot figure out why. I am sure we all do this to some extent. We all have our biases, so I try to keep this instinct in check and think about other points of view. Here are some of the things I try not to dismiss:

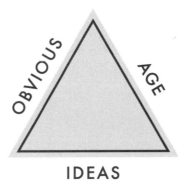

Obvious

Sometimes we need to listen to the obvious because, well, it's obvious. There are times we must rely on common sense, because frequently the "obvious" is simply the truth. This is particularly true when we place what we want to be true against what we know to be true. Will that second helping of dessert have a consequence? Come on, the answer is obvious whether I want to hear it or not. Most of listening to the obvious is listening to the facts. I cannot ignore facts hoping for the decision I want and ignoring the decision that is so obviously the right one.

It's obvious that your industry will change in some way over the next five years. It's obvious we will all grow older each year and have to change some of our habits as a result. It's obvious that we will make mistakes and fail at certain things we try. And instead of dismissing these things, I choose to be prepared for them.

I will be prepared for change and try to get ahead of it where I can. I will try to watch what I eat and be more focused on health as I get older. I will be mentally prepared to learn from and move on from the mistakes and failures I may experience. I will simply prepare for the obvious and not treat it as a surprise when it happens. In order to do that, I must keep my antennas up, my focus sharp, and my thirst for knowledge high.

Age

I know some people who automatically dismiss those who are younger than they are or who are new to their company. Some believe there is no possible way that a younger person can know more than they do. Of course, the opposite can be true as well. Some people dismiss those who are older as outdated, outmoded, or old school. Such attitudes are, to me, very limiting and self-centered.

Many of us go to our children when we have technology issues. In my family's case, Jake knows a heck of a lot more than I do. It would be foolish not to use the knowledge I have at my disposal. Just because he's younger doesn't mean I can't learn from him.

The same can be said about players. The game of basketball is so fast paced that even coaches don't see or hear everything that's going on. In the NBA, during a time-out the head coach will often ask the players what they are seeing or what coverage they feel would work best. They're playing the game, so wouldn't we want their input?

At the other end of the spectrum, we would be foolish not to learn from those who have come before us, those who have learned lessons on their way up, who have made mistakes and learned from them, those who have figured out how to become champions. This is a philosophy I have lived by and that has served me well—learning from the older people in my profession. I have learned to *seek wisdom from those who came before me.*

They have already walked the paths that you are navigating now. They have already had the success that we are working hard to reach and have already experienced the failures we may not know exist. We all want to study the success of others in our line of work, but it is equally important to know the failures they experienced so that we can be on the lookout for them and know how to handle them before they throw us off track. We can use the ideas, strategies, and characteristics of those who passed before us to get where we want to go. And maybe we can even get there faster and better.

I believe that success leaves these footprints. And if we want to achieve our life's goals we have to:

- Find them
- Follow them
- Fit them

We have to *find* the people who have been successful in our field. We have to look outside our field to find others who have employed a strategy that could apply to our needs or a characteristic that we lack.

Once we find them we have to *follow* them. By this I mean study them. We need to read their books, watch their videos, study interviews with them—anything that can help us dig deeper into why they are successful.

The last step is crucial, yet many people don't give it enough attention. Some think once they get the information they can just copy it. It doesn't work that way. Not everything someone else does *fits* the way you do things, fits your personality, or fits your value system. Study what others have done, and extract only what feels the best fit for you. There's not a right way. But there is a way that is natural to who you are. You're not stealing someone's shoes, you're walking in their footsteps.

Ideas

Be careful not to dismiss the ideas that are not your own. Think about all the people who dismissed Henry Ford and that crazy idea of mass-producing cars! Think about all the people who dismissed the Wright brothers and the crazy idea of an airplane! Think about all the people who dismissed three guys working out of their garage—Bill Gates, Paul Allen, and Steve Wozniak—and the crazy idea they had called a computer! How many *ideas* have we failed to take seriously that proved transformational?

I can think of a young assistant coach with the Golden State Warriors, Nick U'Ren, who suggested a change in strategy as the team went into game four of the 2015 NBA championship finals. The Warriors were down two to one in the series when U'Ren, a twenty-eight-year-old, behind-the-bench assistant coach, suggested to Steve Kerr that they change their starting lineup and insert Andre Iguodala in place of Andrew Bogut.

Two things struck many observers. First, this was the NBA finals! Teams seldom change anything that got them there in the first place. Second, the suggestion came from a twenty-eight-year-old who sat behind the bench! Surely Steve Kerr would not listen to such an idea! But he did not dismiss it. Instead he gave the idea thought and decided it made total sense. The rest is history, as that lineup change was a big part of Golden State coming back and winning the title. And Andre Iguodala became the Finals MVP.

That willingness to listen and not to automatically dismiss ideas is part of why Steve Kerr is always in the discussion as the best coach in the NBA. He does not dismiss things that others might. In this case, he did not dismiss age and he did not dismiss an innovative, even radical idea. That idea contributed to winning an NBA championship!

THREE BATTLES

COMBATTING FEAR, FAILURE, AND LIMITATION

I had the privilege of speaking to more than ninety companies and sports teams in 2017, and as I talked to coaches, players, employees, and corporate leaders, I found that even though we all talk a good game, deep down we all put self-imposed mental roadblocks in our own way. I have done it. You have done it. Even the most visible and successful people have done it.

We engage in negative, silent self-thought. We almost stop ourselves before we start. We nearly assure ourselves of the negative before we even give something a chance to play out. We often know all the reasons why we won't succeed before we put forth the effort to see if we can succeed. All of these are roadblocks we put in front of ourselves. And we can control them.

So how do we combat these roadblocks? What are the first steps in getting to greatness? The answer gets back to the second of the Three Sets we must master: mindset. I believe getting to greatness is a mindset that looks like this:

- Our *trust* must be greater than our fears.

- Our *belief* must be greater than our doubts.

- Our *resolve* must be greater than our failures.

- Our *preparation* must be greater than our limitations.

I have found that our most self-destructive beliefs are often self-imposed thoughts on fear, doubt, failure, and our perceived limitations. We think all four of these will forever keep us from becoming successful.

After reading this list you may be filled with more doubts. Can I overcome all of these? Can I overcome any of them? I would say that you can—because all four are things we control simply by what we do and how we think each day.

Trusting yourself, believing in yourself, having a resolve, making sure you prepare well—these are all things you control. You have a say in how these things appear in your life. You can create a mindset in each of these areas to give yourself the best chance of succeeding.

Jon Gordon, the bestselling author, often says, "We need to talk to ourselves much more often than we listen to ourselves." When we listen to ourselves it is almost always a series of self-limiting thoughts. But when we talk to ourselves, we have the power to frame that conversation inside our heads. This is where we can insert more positive thoughts.

But there is a critical distinction in this concept of talking to yourself. If all you ever do is positive self-talk, *nothing* gets done except that it sounds good in your mind. Success is not about what sounds good, it's all about the work you must put in to make it come to life. If your self-talk is never put into action, chances are you are falling farther behind your competitors and continuing to frustrate yourself.

Your talk has to include an "if." I know I am capable of doing this *if* I do the following three things. This is what separates you from many others, because the if is the work that is required—sometimes lots of it! Think of the word "IF" as an acronym for "Intentionally Forward." It's a trigger that leads me immediately to the thought that *if* I believe I can do this, then I must *intentionally* move *forward*.

Let's look at each of the four mindset musts for getting to greatness.

Trust in Yourself

This is not an easy thing to do, but it is doable even if you haven't experienced much success in life. I always go back to what I can control. Where I have been able to develop trust in myself is in meticulous preparation and organization. I feel if I prepare in the best way I can, then I go into anything knowing I have done my best to be ready.

There is comfort in preparation. I understand that not everything will turn out exactly as I hope, but I have trust in what I have done prior and what I will do during. It could need meticulous research. It may require extra work. It may demand sustained thought. And I may need to repeat all of the above many times, but I will give everything that is required. That is what allows me to trust that I am ready to give my best shot!

Believe in Yourself

Believing in yourself, like trusting yourself, comes from all of the work you put in behind the scenes. Success is not automatic. The competition is practicing and preparing too. You are not the only one who wants to succeed. My belief comes from knowing I have done all I can to be the best I can be for whatever it is I am trying to accomplish.

I have found that when hard work precedes trust and belief, you have the opportunity to overcome fear and doubt. Will there always be a little bit of both? Chances are the answer is yes, but don't think you are in the minority. Many successful people still have a little bit of doubt, a little bit of fear. I remember Chris Paul, an all-star, coming into my office after the end of the season and saying, "You may not know it, but I lost confidence at points in the season." Even all-stars face confidence dips.

Resolve

Some may call it resilience. Whichever word you use, the important thing is that you have to develop it. Think back to all the mistakes you made when you were younger, failures you may have had along the way. You are still functioning. You are still alive. You still have a job. My point: you eventually got past it.

I get back to a universal truth. All successful people have failed and made mistakes. Failure is part of life. Mistakes are part of growth. It's what we decide to do after the setbacks, how we react to the setbacks that are the separators of success or failure.

I clearly remember the 2006/2007 Boston Celtic team that finished 24-58. Doc Rivers heard heckling fans and saw articles in the papers questioning whether he was still the best coach for the team. Even with these seemingly daily questions about his ability, Doc never wavered. He was disappointed after every loss, but he kept his job front and center at all times. His job was to coach the team, to motivate the team, and to keep the team a cohesive unit. He did all three. And the following year, because of this resolve, we won the NBA World Championship!

Doc continued to believe in his system, his knowledge of the game, and his ability to coach, because it was based on years and years of work, thought, study, adjustment, and trial and error. His resolve came from his belief in himself and his knowledge. He understood he was hired to do a job, not complain about a job and certainly not blame others.

I remember one conversation when I commented on the way the fans were responding. His reply was immediate and emphatic. He said, "No, this is exactly what we want. They deserve to boo and demand better basketball and winning more games. That shows they care. And I would rather know that the fan base cares about winning basketball than to be somewhere that doesn't." This was a great learning experience for me as a relatively new coach at the professional level. Expectations are good. They keep you on task. They are positive in nature if we see them in the right light!

Work as hard as you can, believe in what you are doing and why you are doing it. Show resolve by digging in a little deeper, dissecting the film a little more, talking with players a little longer. Do the work. That is how you bounce back. Resolve, if given effort, is what beats failure every time. Failure only has the shelf life you allow it to have.

Preparation

You have seen preparation as a central theme of this book for good reason. If you prepare yourself and your team as well as you are capable, you will always have the chance to succeed, and you will always have what is most important as a leader: the respect of the team.

I had the chance to visit the Miami Dolphins in the spring of 2015 when Lawrence Frank and I went to learn about how they ran their operation. We were always trying to learn what other teams were doing to see if we might encounter other ideas we could learn from to improve our own outcomes. The Dolphins' executive vice president of football operations, Mike Tannenbaum, gave us total access, as he is a learn-it-all type himself. He brought us onto the practice field to observe one of the morning sessions. He said he wanted to introduce us to Dan Marino and Peyton Manning.

As Lawrence and I were peppering them both with questions about what made them the players they were, Peyton mentioned his preparation was vital to his success as a player. He said that he had some limitations (even professional athletes do), so his preparation had to be that much better. You may not be Peyton Manning, but you can be like him and not see limitation as a dead end, but as a detour. There is another route to get to the same place. Peyton went the route of preparation.

Trust, belief, resolve, and preparation are the best ways to combat fear, doubt, failure, and limitations every time.

THREE INGREDIENTS FOR SUCCESS

RESPECT, TRUST, LIKE

As I look at some of the best teams I have coached, played with, or observed, they all had three ingredients that allowed them to separate themselves from others. These three qualities created the closeness and connection that is critical to winning at the highest level.

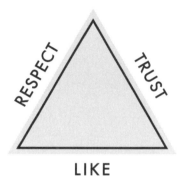

It's the third one on this list that tends to create problems for people. I can hear the popular refrain already: "I don't care if someone likes me or not as long as they respect me." And I understand where that statement comes from. This cliché has been around for so long that I think it has been given a free pass as being the only way to look at team dynamics. But I believe as times change so, too, can the way we look at things, and so, too, can the ingredients that allow a team or organization to separate themselves from the pack. That is where I believe the concept of "like" comes in. "Like" has been discounted for too long. I just ask that you be aware of this aspect of the triangle.

I saw firsthand how the absence of "like" caused someone who looked like he had a promising career to lose that opportunity. If you were to ask around if people respected this person's knowledge of the job, the answer would have been a resounding *yes*. If you asked if people trusted him from the start, you would have also gotten a *yes*. If you asked around if people liked him, the overwhelming majority would have said *no*. This cost him. When he was involved in an incident that led to discussions about letting him go or keeping him, the fact that he wasn't *liked* by colleagues was just too much for him to overcome. I do believe that if he had been well-liked, he may have had an opportunity to survive the incident.

It does not take that much more to live your life in such a way that you can be liked. At the root of being liked is being courteous, which includes commonsense things like saying please and thank you, just like your mom taught you. Being "liked" comes from showing your appreciation for other people, being kind and helpful, not coming across as a know-it-all, showing respect, thinking about others' feelings, and engaging in the group instead of trying to stand out. In other words, all the things you were taught in kindergarten.

We all know how important respect and trust are to advancing in a career, but do not put likeability on the back burner. Remember the triangle of success is three parts: respect, trust, and like. Having all three parts will take you much farther for much longer than just having only one or two parts of the triangle! Trust is a cornerstone of every championship organization, and when coupled with respect and people liking each other, your organization can be poised for success.

It's what I call the "The Success Triangle." Let's take a look at it in the context of a sports team. The triangle is most powerful when it is made up of four relationships:

- The players respect, trust, and like the other players.
- The players respect, trust, and like the coaches.
- The coaches respect, trust, and like the players.
- The coaches respect, trust, and like the other coaches.

When all four of these relationships are strong—because they include respect, trust, and like—the team has the best chance to excel.

The triangle doesn't just apply to the players, as I have seen teams and organizations not reach their potential because the coaches were not aligned. And trust me, players will see this.

As for respect, echoing that earlier statement, I get many an argument that "I don't have to like someone to respect someone." Speaking personally, I have a hard time respecting someone I don't like. It may just be me, but that's my reality. I may respect the work that gets done by some people, but if I don't respect the way they go about doing it, I cannot give them my total respect.

THREE INS

ALL-IN, NOT-IN, GIVE-IN

We all want the same thing from our team or organization. We all want buy-in. But there's a formula for getting a buy-in. It just doesn't happen on its own. Buy-in is a step-by-step process that includes:

- Belief
- Trust
- Truth

In order to get buy-in we must first get "believe in." I am not going to buy into anyone I don't believe in. In order to get "believe in" we must first develop trust. I am certainly not going to believe in someone I don't trust. And in order to trust someone, I have to know that the trust is built on the truth. There is no way I can trust someone who does not tell the truth and does not live the truth.

Buy-in is not the only "in" we must be aware of if we want to have a successful team. There are other "ins" that have a direct bearing on the team's success or failure. Every team looks at the "end game" first and foremost. How much profit do we want at the end of the year? How much growth? Will we be successful if we don't win a championship? However, the "end game" should not be the only game evaluated. Equally as important is the "in-game." The in-game has three areas we must monitor.

All of us want a team that is "all-in." Everybody is all in on how we operate and what we believe. "All-in" groups have a chance to achieve their goals.

None of us want a team filled with members who are "not-in." This type of team has no shot at success. These teams are destined to fail.

But there's a third "in" that not many people talk about but one that is damaging to the success of any team. That is the "give-in." These are the team members who tease us. They are "in" at times and not quite "in" at others. They don't go as far as showing themselves as "not-in," but they aren't totally "all-in" either. These are the people who often try to trick their way into the good graces of leadership and teammates. These are the ones who talk in whispers and hide in the corner and speak up only when the leaders are not around. The "give-ins" are usually motivated by selfish intent, not team intent.

They say things like "Ok coach … what do you want me to do … I'll do it!" But then their actions say, "I'll do it just to get you off my ass, and as soon as I'm out of eyesight I'm going back to my *not-in* mode." "Give-ins" are dangerous because of the selfish attitude they bring and because they are always trying to persuade teammates to join them.

Needless to say, the "end game" has to be the final goal, but the "in" game has to be monitored at all times as that is the pathway to the goal. We don't arrive without the proper "ins"!

THREE UPS

SHOWING UP, SHUTTING UP, KEEPING UP

The players at the Nike's Lebron James Skills Academy were elite high school and college basketball players. Each day as we coached them, the same question kept popping into my head: This group, because of their pure, superior athletic talent, had received a huge opportunity simply by being selected to participate in the academy, but what about the rest? How do others, the ones who might still be developing or the ones in overlooked programs or those simply missed by evaluators, how do they get their "break"?

I was talking about this with Jay Bilas (ESPN college basketball analyst) who was helping us coach the group. Jay said that, in his opinion, a big part of getting a break is "just showing up." His words were like a two-by-four to my head. Immediately I thought about my life and why I was so fortunate to have had the career I have had. To give ourselves a chance for that break we have to "show up."

But there's more to it. Just as important as showing up is that we then have to "shut up" and listen. Plus, we have to "keep up." Shutting up and keeping up are equally important to giving ourselves a chance to succeed.

Showing up

Showing up starts with giving all of yourself all the time, treating every practice and every work day as important. Then you have to show up to place yourself in the company of people you want to meet or the people you want to emulate or those from whom you can learn. For me, showing up always meant being the first one there and the last one to leave. It meant attending coaching clinics, working at summer camps. I seized every opportunity. It got to the point that people said, "Man, that guy's everywhere." What they saw was someone really into coaching and eager to learn. My hustle to gain knowledge and learn from experts got me into the environments where I could learn the most, and along the way, I started developing a reputation as a serious, committed coach.

Shutting up

Shutting up is simply an understanding that you don't know it all. Use your ears more than your mouth. I learned that when I spoke, the only things I heard were things I already knew. I needed to know what other people knew. That is why my ears and eyes became four of my biggest learning tools. My personal philosophy has always been to go through life with big eyes, big ears, and a small mouth. Look and learn. Listen and learn. And keep my mouth shut as I learn!

Keeping up

Keeping up is all about making sure that once you hear something you then invest the time to learn it. After that, you need to put newly acquired knowledge into your life, continue to evaluate it, and make sure you are using it to your best advantage. You *learn*, and then you *study*, you *implement*, and you always *evaluate*. Just because you heard it or saw it doesn't mean you know it. Keep up with the trends in your business, the best practices of your competitors, the best examples of what others are doing. Only then might you get your "break."

This learning process happened to me when I first entered the NBA. I was scared to death because I had not played in the NBA, and I was a true rookie coach again, from my lack of knowledge to my lack of relationships in the business. I just had to keep my mouth shut and learn every day. Then I would stay up every night in order to keep up: to think about and internalize what I learned that day until I knew it so well I gained confidence.

I thought about what Jay Bilas had taught me, and I now live my life with the strategy of showing up, shutting up, and keeping up!

CHAPTER 5

The Power of Lists

1. VALUES

2. OVERCOMING THE OVERWHELM

3. INSIDE THE ROOM

4. PERSONAL SUCCESS PLAN

5. CHAMPIONS ARE ABOUT ...

6. LEAVE A JOB OR LEAVE A LEGACY?

As I said in Chapter 1, I carry several lists in my briefcase, and I frequently pull out my blue folder and study them while I am on a flight or while waiting for a meeting to begin. I have found them to be powerful tools to keep me on task.

Before I go into the lists that have helped me over the years to get to where I wanted to go, accomplish the things I set out to accomplish, and live the life I have always dreamed of living, let me provide the why behind the lists I present in this chapter.

For me, success is all about the habits we have built. And "built" is the operative word. I had to build them from scratch. I had to find out what were the habits used by the most successful people, and then I had to build them in me.

To establish a habit, I need to be consciously thinking about it every day. I know my brain and how it works and, unfortunately for me, my brain is always on, always thinking. And "thinking" for me does not always translate to "remembering." So I did what made sense for me. I created lists that I could carry with me and study. I call these my "Success Lists."

What lists do I currently carry with me? Some are the lists you will encounter in this chapter and others you have already seen within "Success Triangles." But the value of lists is in making them, studying them, and applying them. I would encourage you to consider using these lists for your own success journey. They have been a vital part of my own journey. Then make some of your own!

VALUES

Collège basketball was hit hard by the 2017 FBI cheating investigation, and unfortunately, this has put a negative spotlight on the sport. Knowing so many coaches and having spent all of my professional life in the game, I believe this investigation is not reflective of what is happening in the majority of programs. Basketball has taught me so much about life and has given me so much in terms of valued relationships and access to cherished mentors that I hate to see how the actions of a few are tainting many people's perceptions of the game.

Instead of those few, I think of the overwhelming majority of coaches I know in all sports who lead a values-based life and make values-based decisions. If you were in the sport on a daily basis and not relying only on what the media report, I strongly believe you would see this investigation as I do. The vast majority of coaches follow the rules set by the NCAA and want only to do the best for their student athletes.

As hard as it was to first read about the investigation, at the same time I am encouraged by the fact that, if these accusations are proven to be true, the response may be to clean up recruiting practices and serve as a harsh deterrent for anyone thinking of circumventing the rules in the future. Unfortunately, we all know there will always be those who look for the easier way and make the decision to cheat. My hope is that, with the federal government's involvement in enforcing these rules, those contemplating cheating will think long and hard before they go down that path. Like all sports, basketball needs to follow the lead of those who take the high road, not the low road.

It is impossible to think about this investigation without contemplating the word "values." What a powerful word this is, and what a big part of what was missing in these accusations.

My contention is that if those who have been accused of circumventing NCAA rules had an ethics-based value system they sincerely believed in and lived by, they would have had something to guide them as these situations presented themselves. I have always believed that values are most critical when difficult challenges and situations of right and wrong are put before us. What often happens when people choose "wrong" is that the pressure to win is too great, the money is too significant, notoriety is too tempting, or it's just easier and faster to do it the wrong way. But if you have a strong values system, and your values are part of who you are and how you live, then your values become the lens through which all decisions will be made. They provide the needed clarity to make the right decision.

No matter what position we hold, title we have, or craft we are pursuing, our values are what must stay front and center. Today's world is so competitive and ever-changing that the increasing pressures to succeed will always be there to tempt us. But I believe these types of choices are temporary and that the truth will ultimately come out.

I encourage everyone reading this book to complete an exercise that I recently did for myself and will return to from time to time. Write down everything you value. Create a list and keep it with you as a reminder of what you stand for. What should you include on this list? That depends on your definition of the word "values." For me it is pretty simple but very powerful: A value is something that I am willing to be fired over and/or vigorously and personally fight for!

I list my own values in two categories:

- Those that serve as my guide in times of challenge and times that require difficult decisions.

- Those I must live for others who are part of my life and that I look for in others I choose to be around.

I have written my lists in such a way that they apply to individuals, but I also encourage teams in the sports and business worlds to go through this exercise together. Collectively, what are the things that you value in a teammate? What are the things you value in a leader? What are the things you value in terms of the physical commitment you have to make to your craft? What are the things you value when things are not going so well for the team? In essence, create your own "team lens" to help guide you through the answers to these questions.

OVERCOMING THE OVERWHELM

We all experience those days or weeks where there is just so much coming at us that we almost feel paralyzed. You know you need to do *something* but you don't know *which* something. And we pressure ourselves with a constant reminder that we have more to do and need to do it better!

We all get overwhelmed. We all have a longer list of things to do than we have time in the day. We all feel everything is important. We all want to do everything right now so we can get on to the next thing.

I felt the pressure cooker when I became the vice president of basketball operations for the Los Angeles Clippers. About a week into the job, I realized I had to have an organized plan not only in order to get everything done, but equally as important, to fight the feeling of being constantly overwhelmed. I was fine with admitting my feelings (to myself), but I needed to have a game plan for when that overwhelming feeling crept in.

Whether they admit it or not, this happens to all leaders. The important difference is in what we do about it. I came up with this list to guide me:

- Keep the Main Thing the Main Thing.
- It's about Priority Management—Not Time Management.
- Make Time—Don't Find Time.
- Plan Your Day—Don't Just Show Up Today.
- Make Decisions—Don't Just Shuffle Paper.
- Extend the Game.
- Make Time to Think.
- Simplify, Simplify, Simplify.

Keep the Main Thing the Main Thing. It's always about what is most important and I work hard to tackle and complete that first. This takes discipline and focus.

It's about Priority Management—Not Time Management. My priorities are all about what I need to do, not what I want to do. I structure my day with my priorities placed in my schedule first. Then I build in anything else I want to get done.

Make Time—Don't Find Time. We are always saying: "I can't find the time." I learned a long time ago that I will never find time, so now I only concern myself with the concept of making time. I make time to read. I make time to think. I make time to exercise. The more you make time the more you get things done.

Plan Your Day—Don't Just Show Up Today. I plan my day the same way I planned a practice when I was coaching. Build a schedule that you can sustain. Start the day with a plan.

Make Decisions—Don't Just Shuffle Paper. This is a reminder to me that decisions are part of each day. I need to do my due diligence and then make the decision. Period.

Extend the Game. This is a saying in sports that means you have to get more out of the clock. In basketball we may foul an opponent so they have to shoot free throws and then we get the ball back with no time having come off the clock. I do the same thing now. If I have more to pack into a day, I may get up at 4:00 a.m. and not 5:00 a.m., extending my day.

Make Time to Think. We can't make quality decisions unless we put quality thought into them. Don't get caught on the treadmill of the workday, make time to think. Good decisions are a priority for success.

Simplify, Simplify, Simplify. For me, simplification takes away a lot of the hesitation I get with complexity. Complexity causes doubt; doubt causes hesitation; hesitation hurts productivity.

INSIDE
THE ROOM

T his list is simple yet powerful. It is a reminder to me that when I enter any meeting or discussion, I am going to do all I can to make sure that I am:

- The most prepared person in the room.
- The best listener in the room.
- The best question-asker in the room.
- The best note taker in the room.
- The most respectful person in the room.

The one on this list that I find many people are not prepared for is being the best *question-asker*. My philosophy has always been that I need to get the best information and the deepest answers, so I have to make sure my questions elicit the best responses.

I believe this about questions:

- The quality of your questions determines the quality of your information.
- The quality of your information determines the quality of your knowledge.
- The quality of your knowledge determines that quality of your decisions.
- The quality of your decisions determines the quality of your success.

The most important thing to think about is this: What will the other participants in a meeting see and hear from you? Two questions I always ask myself when I leave the room are:

- Did I represent myself to the level of the standards I demand of myself?
- Did I check every box on my "Inside the Room" list in order to get the most out of the meeting?

PERSONAL
SUCCESS PLAN

As we look at what we do each day, one question has to be at the forefront of our thoughts. What am I intentionally going to do that will help me to grow, develop, and improve? The answer to this question is how you will frame each day, and it will form your "will-do" list. If we are truly operating intentionally, more than being a list of what you "do" each day, it will become your list of what you must make sure you *get from* each day.

This is how I try to get the most out of each day:

- Read (two or more hours each day)
- Think
- Work out
- Keep a "WILT" (What I Learned Today) list
- Have my antennas up
- Produce today—Prepare for tomorrow
- Help the Helper—Give Back

As you look at this list you may ask: What about family? What about sleep? What about work? Obviously, I do not disregard these areas, as they are things that must be given quality attention. This list is directed at my own personal growth:

Read. When I read I grow. Reading has provided me answers, strategies, and ideas I may not have considered had I not read.

Think. Creating "Think Time" allows me to slow down the pace of a hectic day, find quiet time with my thoughts, and ultimately bring more clarity to all that I am doing now as well as all that I hope to do in the future.

Work Out. Working out is tiring for sure, but it actually wakes me up. It provides me more energy to do all I want to do in a day. The days I don't work out seem to coincide with the days I get tired earlier.

WILT List. WILT stands for "What I Learned Today." I do a lot of reading, thinking, observing, and listening each and every day. What comes with that are new ideas, new terms, new potential strategies, new ways to look at things. One of my goals is to try to learn something new each day. So, I came up with what I call my "WILT" notebook. I have a goal to make sure I have at least one new entry every day.

Have My Antennas Up. This is about always having my learning and growth antennas up for opportunities to learn. It heightens my awareness of what is being done and said around me, and of opportunities I can seize that will help me grow.

Produce Today—Prepare for Tomorrow. This is my reminder to accomplish something and get something from each day. It's also a reminder to not leave tomorrow to chance or luck.

Help the Helper—Give Back. So many people have helped me on my way up that I want to do the same for others. I am constantly responding to people who are looking for help, asking me what they can do to get to where they want to go. Someone helped me and I am going to repay that helper by helping others. Helping others is part of my definition of personal success.

This is not necessarily a daily "to do" list but more of a success guideline. It's part of my success plan, my way to remind myself that if I follow this plan each day I will be able to continue on my success journey.

CHAMPIONS ARE ABOUT…

There are some simple realities about being on a team that is trying to win a championship. The most important is that you have a choice. You can choose to "collectively sacrifice," or you can choose to be on a "personal agenda." One choice has proven to give you the best chance to compete for a championship. The other is saved for the articles about the teams that *could have* but *never did*, teams that had talent but focused on individual talent and never gelled as a group, teams that should have been in the championship mix but never were.

As members of teams, we do have the freedom of choice, but we will never have the freedom from the consequences of those choices. One consequence of the choice to play "self-centered" basketball is you will never have a chance at winning a championship.

Below is a list I created of a champion's mindset, which explains how champions think:

- Champions are about getting in and getting up ... not giving in and giving up.
- Champions are about pulling together ... not pulling apart.
- Champions are about sacrificing for others ... not creating for themselves.
- Champions are about the team results ... not who gets the results.
- Champions are about finding solutions ... not placing blame.
- Champions are about building one another up ... not tearing one another down.
- Champions are about playing the team way every day ... not their way.
- Champions are about the end result ... not their results.
- Champions are about doing what it takes ... and not just taking what they can get.
- Champions are about being prepared ... not just being ready.
- Champions are about competition ... not putting on a performance.
- Champions are about fighting for the team ... not fighting with the team.
- Champions are about consistency ... and not about doing it one time.
- Champions are about respecting their opponent ... but fearing no one.
- Champions are about execution ... not about doing their own thing.

- Champions are about doing the little things ... not seeing those things as too little.
- Champions grasp the "the concept of every" ... and stay away from "whenever."
- Champions don't get down in adversity ... they get involved in the solution.
- Champions are about giving energy to their team ... not sucking it out of their team.
- Champions are about raising their team's emotion ... not hijacking their emotions.
- Champions are all about winning ... and have no time for "numbers" players.
- Champions are about one agenda ... not their agenda.

Simply put: champions think "we" and will not accept the thought process of "me"!

CHAPTER 6

The Power of a
Two-Letter Word

What happens when you put a small, but powerful, two-letter word in front of the words we have discussed in this book? And what if that word is spelled N–O ... NO! Think about the complete transformation that occurs. Add "NO" to words like "accountability" or "preparation." Think how that simple two-letter word holds the power to destroy all we have worked for, all we wish to stand for, all of our chances to reach success.

The words we have discussed throughout this book are simple words, really. We have heard them all our lives. We may have heard them so often that we have become almost numb to their deeper meanings. But as I have found out over my career, these are the words of many successful athletes, coaches, leaders, teams, and organizations. They have *intentionally* added them to their vocabulary and lived them each day. These words have formed the foundation of their success.

If you ever doubt that, just put that word NO in front of them and see what happens:

- No trust
- No truth
- No good choices
- No quality circles to travel in
- No commitment
- No understanding of change
- No passion, spirit, or heart put into your work
- No curiosity
- No standards to live up to
- No belief in anything

Now apply this same exercise to your team. Where would we be as a team if this list described us? Would you want to be part of a team that went through a season or a company that spent a fiscal year with NO as its mindset?

- What if your team had NO accountability?
- What if your team had NO humility?
- What if your team had NO intentional plan to their days?
- What if your team had NO urgency?
- What if your team had NO values?
- What if your team had NO buy in to you or each other?
- What if your team had NO interest in getting on to the next thing?

This is not the mindset of a champion!

Putting NO in front of these words is when we see how powerful these words actually are and we begin to understand how the elimination of these words in our lives, teams, and organizations can be devastating to our success.

But now think about how the inverse can also be true with some of the words we encounter in our daily lives. What happens when you knowingly place NO in front of words like "settling" or "procrastination?" This addition can suddenly make these words empowering. It all comes down to another word we've discussed—choice. What happens when you *choose* to turn the destructive power of a two-letter word on its head? You have a choice to make about how you use the word NO!

How many times have you done something and immediately afterward said, "Man, that was dumb; I'm never doing that again!" Or you do something that you know is counterproductive to what you want to accomplish, but you do it anyway. This is something I gave a lot of thought to many years ago because I saw it happening time and time again and I experienced it happening to me as well.

So, finally, one day I said "NO!" And I devised a list of the things that I always knew NOT to do but had fallen victim to. This became the list that I call "Know Your Nos." We choose to say no, to seize power, and turn this destructive word into one that helps us attain a champion's mindset:

- **No Settling.** I refuse to settle for anything less than my best!
- **No Stopping.** Failure will not stop me; it will start me on a quest to overcome it!
- **No Procrastination.** I will become a pro at refusing to give in to procrastination!
- **No Excuses.** I refuse to waste time on excuses and instead spend time on solutions!
- **No Regrets.** I refuse to go to my grave with regrets still inside me!
- **No "Me Firsts."** It can never be all about me!
- **No Burned Bridges.** Bridges must be built and maintained, not burned or destroyed!

You won't be surprised to learn that I also made lists for our team. These were things as a team we were going to decide NOT to do. And the more I could get the team to come up with the items on the list, the better buy-in I got from them.

Always remember that the word NO has the power to ruin or the power to help. You just have to choose how you use it.

CHAPTER 7

The Power of
Your Legacy

T he last word I hope you will put serious thought to is legacy. I want to leave you with this word because it is the final piece of the success puzzle. It's not just about having success, it's about what you do with your success that really matters. In my mind, it is important to share that success with others just as others have done in your life.

I started thinking about this word *legacy* many years ago. Like you, there have been times when I've wondered—Why am I doing this? Why am I putting all these hours into my job? Why am I sacrificing so much? My answer was always twofold: I loved what I was doing, and I really wanted to help people get the best from themselves and reach their goals. Could this be my legacy—helping others find success and fulfillment by passing on what I've learned from the best of the best?

Maybe legacy sounds like something too grand or ambitious. But I think of it this way: we leave a legacy through doing our part in our piece of the world. It can be that simple.

LEAVE A JOB OR LEAVE A LEGACY?

If you just want to leave your job after your last day of work, then what you're doing on an everyday basis is probably enough for you to keep your job. But if you want to leave a legacy, then each day of work becomes important. The intent you bring to each day changes. The example you set each day is under greater scrutiny. But most importantly, the lessons you teach those who will follow in your footsteps will be rewarded by their successes.

You leave a legacy by the attitude you bring each day, the example you set, the conversations you have, and the mentoring you do. Your legacy comes from bringing your best every day and by bringing out everyone else's best as well.

I was thinking about the importance of legacy not long ago when I was speaking to teachers and administrators in Yuma, Arizona. The importance of legacy is always within me, but speaking in this atmosphere—in the auditorium of Kofa High School, a place normally filled with students—legacy became dominant in my mind. How can one spend any time in a high school and not think about the opportunities the next generation will have as they start to make adult decisions about their futures?

On that warm Arizona winter day, the auditorium was vacant, seven hundred seats with not a soul in any of them as I thought about legacy and I mentally walked through the talk I was going to give to more than 500 teachers, administrators, and leaders of the Yuma Unified School District. I'm not so different in my preparation from Ray Allen in that I always arrive early to an event, so I can get a feel for the environment, and I want to get my mindset right. I want to look at the empty seats of that room and remember that my talk is all about the audience and not about me. My only job that day was to impact and inspire the people in those seats. I wanted them to leave knowing that there truly is a lot more inside each of them. And if I've done my job, they will leave with new strategies for unlocking the best they have within themselves.

But I knew many in that Yuma audience, despite giving of themselves every day to their students, didn't realize they could leave their own legacy. "All I do is teach," they might say, rather than seeing the fullest possible impact of that teaching. They might think they can only reach a handful of the students they work with each day. In other professions it might be, "All I do is manage a team of fifteen," or "All I do is sell a product." They may think their impact is so small that they can't possibly leave any kind of legacy.

But the power of a legacy has nothing to do with numbers and everything to do with the lessons. It's not the number of people you are in front of each day or the number of minutes you have with them, it's the value of the lessons you leave with those whose lives you touch.

The auditorium was filled with over 500 people, but it could have been just one person and I would have had a chance to work on my legacy. That day I gave three and a half hours to sharing my message about realizing potential and the needs behind achieving success, and as is my habit, I stayed around for as long after as there were people wanting to ask additional questions.

There was one young man who stayed until all the others left. He coached of one of the local high school soccer teams to a state championship, and he wanted to ask me a few questions about how to repeat that accomplishment. We spent fifteen minutes talking about ideas on how to create a repeat mindset in his players. I turned the tables on him and asked about what he had done to achieve the success his team had accomplished. I enjoyed our conversation, was enthused by his passion, and hoped I had helped in some small way.

A few days later, the organizer of the event sent me a copy of an e-mail he had received from that young soccer coach. The coach said that he had met with his mentor and shared some of the things he had picked up from our talk. He said he could not believe I had asked *him* questions about what *he* did to win the state championship. He could not believe that "an NBA championship-winning coach wanted to learn how a high school soccer coach got his team to that level of play."

Here is what his mentor said to him, "One day you will switch places with Mr. Eastman, and you will be enlightening a young future leader with all of *your* knowledge and experiences."

That day in Yuma was a *legacy* day for me. A number of people thanked me and told me how much they got out of my talk, but this one-on-one conversation after I spoke is what I am building my legacy on. It's not so much about how many people you touch, it's about reaching out with intention, it's about caring about other people and wanting to help them realize their dreams. If I could help that young coach, just think how many young lives he can impact. I will chalk that day up as a major success. I did my part in my piece of the world that day. That is how a legacy is built.

I ask that you think about *all* the words and concepts you have spent time with in this book and that you pass on your words and experiences to others. The world may be big, but your legacy is created right where you're standing!

When Words Become Lasting

ll the words and lists that form the heart of this book have been developed by my thinking about the nature of success and by carefully listening to and observing the actions of the best of the best. The words come from a lifetime working alongside those who have excelled in their careers and in their lives. But I don't just want you to think of them as their words or my words, I want you to think deeper and more personally. Think about how the incredible power of these words becomes real for you when you apply them in your life, in your career, at your job, or on your team.

And one final list before we end:

STRENGTH LIES INSIDE EACH OF US

- Start with your heart.
- Analyze with your head.
- Give your gut a say.
- Learn with your eyes and ears.
- Ask probing questions with your mouth.
- Find strength in your mind.
- Be strong in your core.

Start with your heart

I believe in order to be successful your heart must be in it. You have to put your heart into something, because that is the strength separator. Our hearts keep us going. However, heart alone is not a guarantee of success. Doc Rivers always told our teams when we began those incredibly competitive playoff journeys: "Sometimes you have to put your heart into something knowing that it may be broken."

He went on to explain that he has only won one championship title in all the years he has been in the business as a player or coach. His heart has been broken many times. But he picks his heart up and puts it right back into the next season. The investment of the heart is an investment of all champions.

Analyze with your head

Emotion is great, but it cannot be the focal point. Your head must provide the pre-thought and the logic that major decisions demand.

Give your gut a say

I define the gut as the combination of all of my experiences, successes, failures, observations, conversations, and learning. In short, it is the summation of all my days on this earth. Together they add up to this feeling, this educated hunch that needs to be factored into our decisions.

Learn with your eyes and ears

The best way to go through life is with big eyes, big ears, and a small mouth. Observe and learn. And stay quiet so you can concentrate on the lessons.

Ask probing questions with your mouth

To me it's all about what you can learn. What you learn is directly proportional to how much you grow. The way I look at it is this: "I already know what I know, and if all I know is what I know, I don't know enough. I need to know what you know." Use your mouth not so much to talk but to learn. Ask questions. Ask for more depth of information. Ask for more clarification so that you leave with total understanding. We need to keep our mouths shut unless we are using them for growth—either our growth or helping others grow.

Find strength in your mind

Jay Bilas, in his popular book *Toughness*, talks about this thing called mental toughness, and it's not what many people think it is. Your mind is tough when you can say no to a fight. Your mind is tough when you can fight through physical and emotional obstacles. Your mind is tough when you can stay the course even though the course is really, really hard. Doc Rivers used to tell our team that toughness is *not* throwing the punch. It's walking away from the fight. Our minds are as strong as we need them to be, ask them to be, and train them to be.

Be strong in your core

Just as the core of our body must be strong, as everything we do passes through our core muscles, we need to strengthen the mental core that leads us to our growth and success. My core consists of my mind first and foremost. I must learn more to grow more to become more.

The second part of the core for me is my heart. My heart is my filter for right and wrong. Deep down in my heart, I know what is right and wrong for me; that I should work out to stay healthy; that I should never cheat in anything I do; and that I should be kind.

The other core is my discipline. I have to continue to be intentional about discipline. I must continue to make sure discipline beats human nature every time.

If I am strong of mind so that I can continue to learn and grow, if I am strong of heart and let it continue to guide me in right versus wrong, and if I have the discipline to overcome human nature, I feel I can reach almost any goal I set. I can become whatever it is I have always hoped to become. But it starts at the start: the core!

As you leave this book, remember one thing above all else: the best are the best for a reason. Learn from champions how they become champions.

Once you decide what parts of this book fit you or your team, make sure they become who you are in everyday life. These words must be lived, not just used in conversation. The best of the best don't just have them in their vocabulary—they live them each day! Then adopt and adapt; find your own words. And once you have made them who you are, pass them on to the next generation who will one day sit in your seat and be a part of a team just as you are.

Remember that words, if you live them, can:
- Take you to another level in your life.
- Build a sustainable organization.
- Turn a group of people into a team.
- Turn those who do a lot of winning into The Winner.

I believe that words can also:
- Take you from where you are to where you want to go.
- Turn how you currently think to how the best think.
- Take you from having a dream to living your dream.

Your job now is to:
- Take these words from having them in your vocabulary to actually living them.
- Turn an interest in these words to a commitment to these words.
- And as my good friend George Raveling says: Make sure when all is said and done with your life that your gas tank reads EMPTY!

REFERENCES

Ben Bolch, "Blake Griffin suspended for four games, plus pay for one more," *LA Times*, last modified February 9, 2016, http://www.latimes.com/sports/clippers/la-sp-cn-clippers-blake-griffin-suspended-20160203-story.html.

Oren Harari, "Quotations from Chairman Powell: A Leadership Primer," GovLeagers.org, last modified 1996, http://govleaders.org/powell.htm.

Jon Gordon, *The Energy Bus: 10 Rules to Fuel Your Life, Work, and Team with Positive Energy* (Hoboken: Wiley, 2007).

Max Weigand, "Because of 4am: Inside the Mind of Kobe Bryant," Medium, last modified November 8, 2017, https://medium.com/@MaxWeigand/because-of-4am-inside-the-mind-of-kobe-bryant-df2a2e6db28a.

Jim Collins, *Good to Great: Why Some Companies Make the Leap ... And Others Don't* (New York: Harper Collins, 2011).

Sean Glennon, Tom Brady vs. the NFL: The Case for Football's Greatest Quarterback (Chicago: Triumph, 2016).

Zameena Mejia, "Warren Buffer says this one investment 'superceded-eds all others'," CNBC, last modified October 4, 2017, https://www.cnbc.com/2017/10/04/warren-buffett-says-this-one-investment-supersedes-all-others.html.

Anton Tabuena, "UFC 184: Ronda Rousey vs. Cat Zingano Video: Training Day Part 1 – 2," Bloody Elbow, last modified February 24, 2015, https://www.bloodyelbow.com/2015/2/24/8099325/ufc-184-ronda-rousey-vs-cat-zingano-video-training-day-part-1-2.

Kate Torgovnick May, "I am, because of you: Further reading on Ubuntu," TEDBlog, last modified December 9, 2013, https://blog.ted.com/further-reading-on-ubuntu/.

Jon Gordon, "The Best Advice I've Ever Heard," The Jon Gordon Companies, accessed June 6, 2018, http://www.jongordon.com/positive-tip-best-advice.html.

ACKNOWLEDGMENTS

I want to thank my dad, who showed me every day what being caring, kind, and first-class is all about. He was a man of few words but a leader by example. I'm grateful to him for so many things, including his insistence that I do things I didn't want to do—or didn't think were important. I didn't realize that so many of these lessons would shape who I have become as a person and a leader. I guess that was the magic of my dad.

There are so many others to thank:

My high school coach, Dave Wiedeman, who instilled a confidence and toughness in me and showed all of us that we had more inside than we thought.

Doc Rivers, who gave me the opportunity to coach in the NBA and experience winning at the highest level. I learned so much standing next to him every day; his wisdom and guidance have been invaluable.

George Raveling, my mentor and friend. The many talks we've had over the years have been challenging and enlightening. He has showed me that giving is the most important thing one can do in life. I am thankful for the time and wisdom he has invested in me; I am a better person for that. The best way I can thank him is to pass along what I can to others.

My editor, Mark Leichliter, who has made this experience enjoyable and educational. He has given his time, thought, and energy to this project, and I am so fortunate to have had Mark as a teammate on this book.

The championship coaches and corporate leaders who allowed me to personally interview them. Their quotes at the beginning of each chapter are meaningful and thought-provoking, and their wisdom is woven throughout this book.

The many others who have allowed me to ask questions or simply sit at their tables to listen and learn. My thanks to each one of them for sharing their thoughts and experiences with me and with the reader.

And, certainly, I need to say thank you to the two most important people in my life:

My wife, Wendy, who has always been there to encourage me, push me, and tell me the truth. She has taught me more than she knows, or than I will ever admit. Her many talents put me to shame. I am forever thankful that she is my wife and friend.

And my son, Jake, who means more to me than he will ever imagine. He, too, has taught me more than I can express. He makes me proud every day.

ABOUT THE AUTHOR

Over his forty years in the game of basketball at the collegiate and professional levels, Kevin Eastman has become widely known as one of the very best teachers in the game.

He is also a lifelong student of the coaches and players at the highest levels.

As a coach of the 2008 NBA Champion Boston Celtics, Kevin has lived in the world of the best while observing and studying them every day. He studies what makes the best The Best—their habits, mindsets, strategies, and every day choices.

Known as a thought leader in the basketball and sports worlds, and is now an engaging speaker who inspires a wide range of audiences, from college and professional sports teams to diverse corporate and government groups.

Kevin's curiosity and dedication to learning provide the backdrop for delivering powerful talks on leadership, culture, teamwork, and why the best are The Best.

SPEAKING AND CONSULTING SERVICES

K evin's forty years of experiences working in the game with high-performing individuals and championship-level teams are at the core of the lessons and messages he shares. His behind-the-scenes stories captivate and inspire diverse audiences—not just sports fans. His energy, wit, and ability to simplify concepts will leave you with memorable and actionable strategies applicable to your career and your life.

Kevin's work with organizations looking for strategies to develop teamwork, create culture, lead in today's competitive environment, and repeat success have been well received by audiences throughout the United States and abroad. To inquire about a speaking engagement, recent topics, or consulting services, please visit kevineastman.net or email us.

Twitter: @kevineastman
LinkedIn: kevineastman4
Email: kevin@kevineastman.net
Website: kevineastman.net